Alan Wearne | These Things are Real

New Poems

GIRAMONDO POETS

Alan Wearne | These Things are Real

First published 2017
from the Writing & Society Research Centre
at the University of Western Sydney
by the Giramondo Publishing Company
PO Box 752 Artarmon NSW 1570 Australia
www.giramondopublishing.com

Designed by Harry Williamson
Typeset by Andrew Davies
in 10/16.5 pt Baskerville BT

Printed and bound by Ligare
Distributed in Australia by NewSouth Books

National Library of Australia
Cataloguing-in-Publication data:

Wearne, Alan, 1948–
These Things are Real / Alan Wearne
ISBN 978-1-925336-32-0 (pbk)
A821.4

for Laurie Duggan and Martin Duwell

Other poetry books by Alan Wearne

Public Relations
New Devil, New Parish
Out Here
The Nightmarkets
The Lovemakers
The Australian Popular Songbook
Prepare the Cabin for Landing

I tell you
These things are real)
ERN MALLEY 'Le petit Testament'

The people who you think are radicals might really be conservative. The people who you think are conservatives might really be radical.
MORTON FELDMAN (after which he began to sing the opening of Sibelius *5th Symphony*)

'Remember,' Ernie Theobalds continued, 'we have a sense of humour, and when the boys start to horse around, it is that that is gettin' the better of 'em. They can't resist a joke. Even when a man is full of beer, you will find the old sense of humour hard at work underneath it. It has to play a joke. See? No offense can be taken where a joke is intended.'

So the foreman spoke, and everyone believed.
PATRICK WHITE *Riders in the Chariot*

Anyone who thinks he recognises himself in these pages, probably does.
NINO CULOTTA *They're a Weird Mob*

Hail! Muse! et cetera.
LORD BYRON *Don Juan Canto III*

Contents

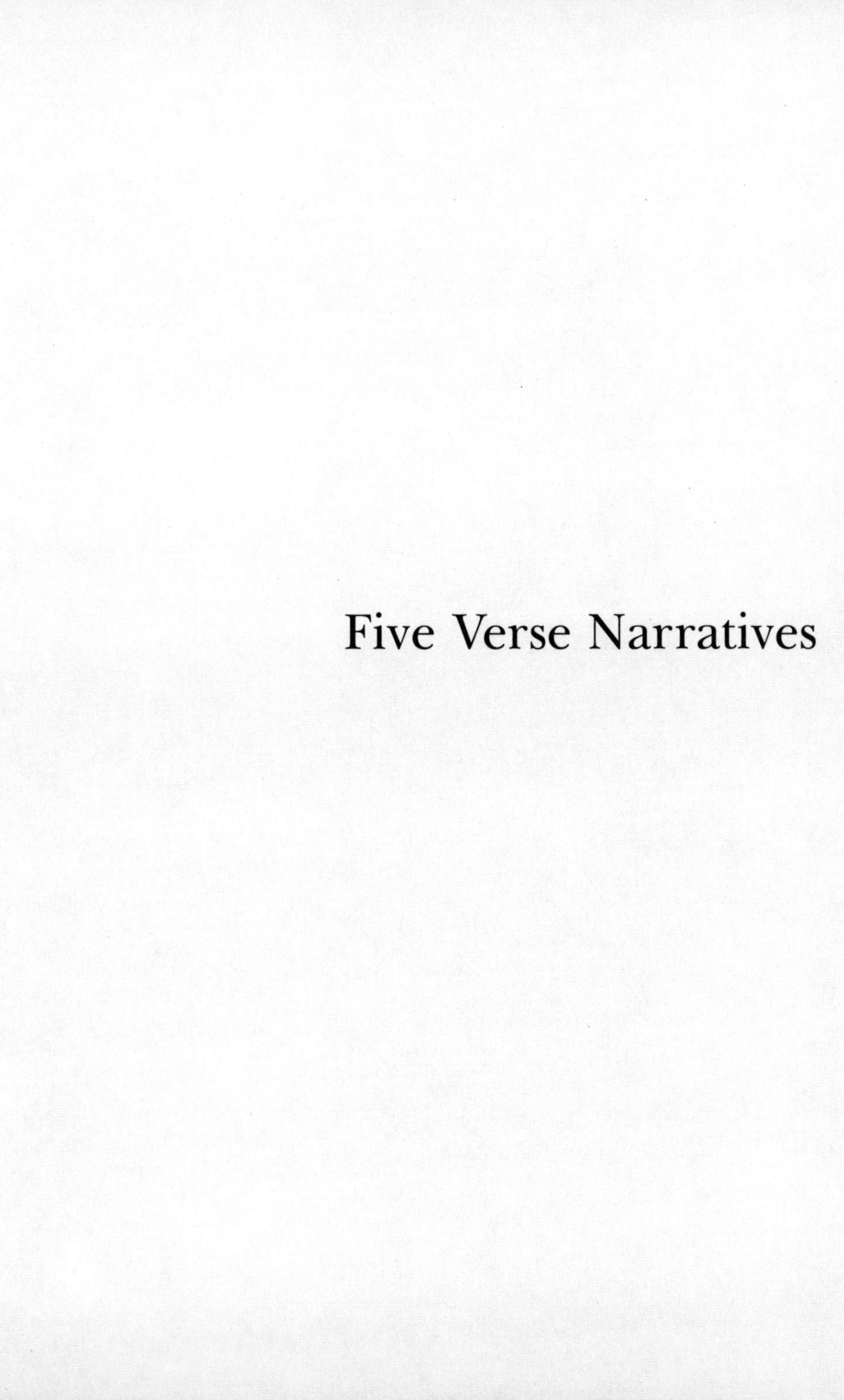

Five Verse Narratives

They Came to Moorabbin

Just after she turned twenty,
when the War was nearly three years old,
Iris joined the AWAS: an adventurous choice
and a sensible one for her, Dot, Elwyn, Gwen,
that generation of unadorned names,
Jean and Elaine, Nance and Wynne.
Later,
at some regimental hop, Iris met Keith,
who fibbed about his age, first to the army
then to her, but who seemed to say
what she considered correct things:
the outline of his plans, for one.
And being adaptable Iris could adjust
(that's what she knew Keith liked in her)
as his plans became their Post-war plans,
and the Post-war plans turned opinions, his opinions,
then reactions, then demands, particularly demands.
And this was when all visits to his brother
(and very soon his mother) ceased.
That same winter,
one mild Sunday afternoon with their three boys
at Half Moon Bay, Iris recognised her:
Nance, Nance Bliss, someone she had slightly known
in Cipher, a mother of four who soon informed
'He died last year, my husband.
You may have known him Iris, from the War,

Tony Conway, who became a diplomat...'

—

That day this trio settled it:
Nance with her minimal desire for charity
but always accepting friendship,
Iris appreciating someone new and interesting,
and Keith (hoping to maintain his need
for being needed) who could be useful:
fixing her taxes for one thing,
whilst the children, hers and theirs,
bound by little more than some trip to the beach,
were courtesy cousins now, friendly
if hardly 'made for each other' friends.
So soon, another Sunday afternoon,
see in that twelve mile trip to Moorabbin
Iris and Keith sensing Nance to be
just that touch removed from their more
'comfortable' friends: the Vineys, the Izzards,
the Dobsons, the Prices.
'I've got over some of it...'
and she was shrugging. 'The children help of course,
but...but...' And the shrugs continued,
leaving her new friends to understand
What else in this woman's life has ever been
so unique? Nothing at all.
Following his funeral Nance knew

she must be playing any amount of roles
(what adjustments wouldn't be required
as a diplomat's wife turned Moorabbin widow?)
for if hers was a roomy, weatherboard villa,
'I'm no Martian,' she'd inform, 'but here I live on Mars.'

    Tony's death must belong to Nance,
who else need wallow in it?
Once you felt sorry for any others feeling sorry
for you, where then would such sorrows cease?
Which was why she took to them:
Iris and Keith knew her, Nance, not Nance and Tony,
and a new small part of her life could now commence.
It had to, even if Keith would greet
'Hi Toots!' and farewell 'Bye Toots!' so half of Mars
would hear him.
                    If she's my age knew Iris
that much more has happened to her:
wartime and beyond when so many women saw
death demanding of their men:
'Now you're marching off with us.'
Which hadn't yet been Keith.
                                        Nance she recalled,
came from a different crowd to hers
(and Dot, Elwyn, Gwen and Wynne's).
Here was a woman good (or much too good?)
with men, so that when Corporal Bliss meets
Major Conway, fifteen years older, divorced,
and set to recommence in External Affairs,

would she like to join him? Yes she would in
Wellington, Edinburgh, Cape Town and Moorabbin,
where he dies.

And where he remains,
trim and balding, shaking hands with Mr Menzies,
framed and mounted on the mantelpiece
(always gets the visitors bemused does Mr Menzies).

First though Nance in her Nance way
will tell her friends: 'My father was a teacher,
his running gag was school inspectors...' and
'If I'm not middle-aged today I'll sure be middle-
aged tomorrow...' and 'Now call me a sophisticate,
but what sophisticate's a Moorabbin sophisticate?'
And then 'If at night,' she won't mind confessing,
'my eldest two should find me teary,
here's hoping they will understand,
although I'm sure the only time death gets understood
is when you've reached there.' She paused and asked herself,
'A bitch? I'm not that touch more bitchier than many but
I have to be, I must, my children need their lives now.'

Later she'd be telling Iris (and only her)
'...his first marriage flopped i.e. little happened.
The War helped close it. When I met him Tony craved
for change, so I gave into the exotic life
of a diplomat's wife. Cape Town and our consulate?
Think proteas and marble floors with staff provided.
And yes there were slivers of glamour,' Nance confided.
'Black nannies to prop the slim young wife-with-martini,

the not so slim young mum with three-make-it-four
in seven years.'
                        Then after Tony got invalided home
they came to Moorabbin where, as a diplomat's widow
you really are exotica and (what a choice!)
either a snob or not.
                        That's where Iris mattered:
you could let loose your hidden snob with her,
who was loyal and never deserved to be a target.
Some week days Nance packed up her youngest two
and drove to this good sport, top scout, great chum
who had the measure of the Women's Pages,
who liked checking the star signs for fun,
who understood all that slapstick potential
chatting with Nance entailed,
who, unlike the Martians knew it was
So nice to have a man around the house...

When as a friend, a visitor or host, Nance hearing Keith
believed him to be the kind of man that she might deal with;
the times were still Post War enough and little seemed
more Post War and less like Mars than Keith:
wanting something to believe in, and how he could transform
beliefs into opinions: the individual and family, his family,
your family and *Know* he'd always emphasise
what you're talking about be it free enterprise growth for
an unlimited Australia, the British Commonwealth of Nations,
or even the Match of the Day, that's right,
Know what you're talking about or failing that

make it perfectly understood one has one's beliefs
(though if one found one had overreached
one might fall back upon *Oh no no no I never said*
exactly that!).

Though *Iris,* a girl friend wouldn't even
barely ask *why did you marry* him?

And, as if in reply
to such an absent question, this would have arrived
Because that's my enigma, and you or anyone
will never solve it.

'My children,' Nance was asking,
'maybe there's not too much to worry over?
Though imagine if there is I'm hardly certain what.'

'If,' Iris answered, 'your father dies
when you are six (mine did, pneumonia)
you just step around it for you need to...'

Well she's a stoic Nance thought,
though if I sat as she does (ever pleasant ever pleasing)
to marinate in Keith's opinionating,
wouldn't my time be ulcer time!

True, yet something
in the widow thrived with him. That something
also saying *Please never lay a hand on me,*
I'd lose Iris, I'd lose Tony, and if I've had it with
that stuff and you know what is meant by 'that stuff',
in all the variety of mourning this'll be my mourning,
Moorabbin style.

Then Keith started visiting, weekdays

(the taxes and what else) telling Toots
she looked like Lauren Bacall, which was nice.

'I'm no June Allyson,' she mock-confessed,
nor Mitzi Gaynor even less.' True Kay Kendall
might've been auditioned, but with her strong, worldly
wise eyes Betty Bacall sounded fine. 'And why not,' she riffed,
'Celeste Holm or Glynis Johns for Iris?
And if you want a star for Tony, think Trevor Howard:
all that officer's necessity to play it correct
with just a hell-raiser's touch, then possibly not,
probably not, till one day just as surely never.
I loved him, nursed and loved him...' and she
would never love-and-nurse another,
since Nance loathed dying, Tony's dying and sometimes
even him for dying.

And how might Miss Holm or Miss Johns
take to their husbands visiting a certain Miss Bacall?
Sports, scouts and chums (always trusting,
forever understanding) needed to be protected,
Nance knew that much and knew her limits.
Though she could imagine Keith informing Iris how
that afternoon he'd just dropped by Moorabbin
(nothing else for there was nothing else)
and in the telling, enjoying it, allowing his wife
to plain soak up any ambiguity she thought was there,
any envy she might be making out of it.
After which who knew what tensions might result,
what balances have to get regained?

Yet they continued to connect, Keith and Nance,
almost as if they had to, though by now her tragedies,
portrayed as oh-so-matter-of-fact,
helped him in overreacting to his own. Item:
such things as what his brother did,
doing Keith or the mother or both out of some late
great aunt's South Gippsland investment property,
when that place that place should've been heading
his way, since doesn't it come down to this:
it's the individual that always matters,
and given Keith's an individual, lest we forget
all those Little Sir Echoes rising through the ranks
of his party, the *Party of the Individual* and,
Nance must be told, he's sure not one of them
and no (he motions to the mantelpiece)
he and Mr Menzies haven't met, one day though
they might.

How do widows adjust?
Now that interests Iris, adding she trusts to her
understanding;
or enough that she's mentioning to Keith how the daughter
still sleeps with the mother. He though believes his wife
is making such an amount of what, exactly?
She must return to his motto:
Know what you're talking about. Such as this:
when it comes to them, them as a family unit,
he knows she loves him, he has his career,
and with that career, life (their life) has been laid on,

that's fair, isn't it?

There was so much

Iris needn't do!

'She,' Keith might be expounding,

'she doesn't have to do *that*, this one's a daughter of
our mod-con era, doesn't want to, either...'
Because, if you think it over, life today is scarcely what
our mothers went through: Australia is the individual,
the individual is Australia, and hadn't we seen the War
so folks need never think of anything else?

'Possibly,' Nance muttered back to Keith,
Keith speaking for his Iris.

Possibly?

He lets her say it since, except when Iris contradicts,
Keith rather likes an opinionated woman,
each brings out a similar boorish edginess
in the other.

So here comes Nance

(are you ready Keith?) on how this town, their town
their *Goodbye Melbourne Town, Melbourne Town Goodbye*
has or hasn't come of age.

'*Sure in 1926*

the world gets told, if it can be bothered listening,
weren't we some backwater's backwater.
*Now though...*Now though?
Name another thirty years before, name thirty years ahead
and won't we still be saying
Oh my, haven't we caught up!

It's ludicrous all this HSV-7, this XVI Olympiad
bringing the world (the world!) to Melbourne,
let alone Moorabbin: '96, '26, '56, '86 and help us
if we've survived '16. The world?
Tony showed me the world for he was the world.
But now I've seen it like I've seen enough
Moorabbin Martians peeping over and squinting through
my fences. No Keith, I don't require that kind of world:
the one minding everybody's business but its own,
the one that calls how I spend my days *chain-smoking*,
which since Tony left cannot be helped.
And if it's believed I soak my nights in Yalumba,
Aspros and Yalumba, I'll always attend to my kids first,
that's what widows must be for; and if Nance enjoys a man
for conversation, which she does, she does not need you
or any other putting his hand inside her blouse,
now if ever.
And it's not for mere appearances
I am voting *Government*, but ever since nice Mr Menzies
arrived in Cape Town, to puff and speechify about
the consulate, like some school inspector,
I've thought he couldn't run the Village Glee Club.
Okay Keith, you would take him seriously,
but weren't you made for Mr Menzies, President Eisenhower,
the very Duke of Edinburgh: that entire school inspector
common touch? I might vote the way I do although a vote's
the only thing they're getting. Otherwise I'm Bolshie,
platinum Bolshie!' What has he heard? What has Keith heard?

and pausing Nance attempts to rectify with this:
'You too must appreciate it: needing squabbles,
like I need my sherry, my eldest needs his homework.'
    Homework? She shouldn't have said that,
it only gets her knowing and re-knowing that if for some
Post War seems as the very best in years, they're equally the
    worst
for men like Keith who need but catch
(or think they have as no-one else has)
a clear, plain, terrifying word, derailing him alone.
    So what's he heard?
That Nance believes his sons of eight of six of four
never do their homework! Never? He saw to it,
he saw to it!
                    Now this demands perspective,
so let's make this very much one of time and place.
Some of you must recall how every year,
on an early April Saturday, outside any newsagent,
the Sun News-Pictorial announces to Moorabbin,
Moorabbin and all the world IT'S ON AGAIN.
You know that one? Well meet today's equally as special
It's on again, and as Nance knows she doesn't need
one single *It* being *on* let alone *again*
from such as Keith. Hasn't she heard, seen and walked away
from this before: men who are so sure they're
being baited, bailed-up and baited,
till 'Keith' it must be asked, 'what are you hearing?
You overreact to just about the lot...'

(who'll turn away making sure they're hearing nothing).
    And Tony was hardly that.
Nance knew him as an urbane, disciplined man,
who when he discovered he was dying
(with a fourth child still to be born)
set out to find and buy a home his family might
survive him in.
                    But then he was an officer and diplomat.
    Iris too remembers Tony (if hardly knew him)
though she can't tell Keith who won't believe her.
    'That Nance,' he tells his wife and sons,
'sometimes I know she's out to trap me...'
though thriving on their squabbles seems but a way of
letting her know *Watch me get out of this one, Nance!*
True he'll be the paragon family friend: visiting the widow,
taking her eldest to the footy, attending to her taxes,
which being more than mere correct is the only thing
It's decency! to do. Besides, he'll never have to live
    with her.
    Might these have been our weak-willed years?
Perhaps, though post any war won't plenty surely wish
to opt for a complacent life? And might these easily
have been our strong-willed years, propped for many
by that vigilance we fought for?
    And there between both weak and strong wills
Iris makes her stand: 'Shall we return to Half Moon Bay?'
    'Let's not,' she's told.
                              The wife suggests

a bigger house, to which her husband gets annoyed:
'All right all right we'll get one, one day...'
And with his eldest soon for the Boy Scouts,
Nance's soon for Highett High School,
since he's back on Mars again, let's make Martian fun,
spruiking like some HSV-7 barker:
'Mr Taxman says *Anytime is Tax Time!*'
And no need gloating
but how more democratic can a nation get
than when Mr Menzies and his *Party of the Individual*
wins yet again?
Though beyond all this, Toots,
no-one must find fault with Iris, his Iris
(did she understand?) although Toots guesses that
each day to her face he's finding fault and faults
and she's guessing right.
On their next visit Iris takes another stand,
her own small, tentative view
on what a woman such as Nance might do.
'Oh...' sighs Keith and 'Oh...' her husband whines,
'as if you'd bloody know!'
Never was Iris
more her friend than then, with Nance appreciating
she couldn't do a thing, realising that
Though I can understand you, Keith,
I'll never know how I'm to deal with you,
you with your need to be required
(made as much for widows as for wives).

Who some days later is out there in her kitchen,
yet again announcing: 'Taxes, Toots, taxes coming up!'
And as her mouth starts and continues drying
Nance rehearses *For all your repertoire of Toots,*
of Betty Bacall, your wife is my friend
and you will never speak to her like that
in front of me again. Which rehearsal never will be
acted out, for if there is a Keith she can't predict,
much worse there's one she can:
that tension in those men wishing *they* had been
the officers, who know they'll never be the diplomats
shaking Mr Menzies' hand.
If a canny friend had heard and seen
what Iris copped, she may have given her that slightest glance
which read *Can't help himself? Oh yes he can!*
Though it's the that even cannier Nance who asks herself
If I follow through and take him truly take him on,
where would such a declamation pay out?
She's answering *On his wife.*

——

There'll still be tolerance,
a ten-year tolerance bringing Iris, Keith and the boys
to Moorabbin, but it's a fading tolerance,
for Nance will stop her understanding Keith,
except as someone still producing his portion of
their mutual grit; and for a bonus getting herself to believe

Wasn't it enough he kept his hands away from me
and did my taxes? Somebody had to.
Till one day
that Keith having his fill of *that Nance*
(someone Iris recalled from AWAS,
someone she met at the beach) leaves and won't return.
All that remains are cards,
the annual women's ritual of greeting cards,
which finishes when Iris dies;
after which Keith climbs into his car not just to fade
but vanish with some ageing bowling club girlfriend
no-one guessed he had.
With or without Mr Menzies
Tony has been stored away and Nance is telling her family:
'Let me leave Moorabbin, leave it to the Martians...'
which she does and how she ends,
tubed-up for emphysema, a granny in a granny flat,
out the back of her daughter's.

Anger Management: a South Coast Tale

If, in single motherhood there's chaos,
some days though are blessed, some days
to make you think *I like what I am seeing*
even (especially) the stubble and the sweat
this Saturday morning where,
swaying outside the supermarket, doubtless slightly stoned
he's busking.
And you want to talk to him,
find out where he's from and where he's staying.
Couldn't the town add more like him
to its personnel: resentful Leagues Club longtimers,
commuters, developers, the fly-in rich,
uni-bods, the tattooed, the dreadlocked, the mums
and musos.
And as you pay
for what's being played he slips in 'Thanks'
and how there's more this evening at the Bowlo.
You and a girlfriend go of course.
Knowing you and what could start,
she's made damn sure you won't look plain
at all. And if not tonight (yes it's not tonight)
there's going to be one night soon, except it is
one early afternoon, and sooner than you planned,
back at your place you both are talking
(talking plus the rest) well before the kids
get home.

And it's good getting to know him!
Somehow you feel he'll think *Nice children*
and he does. It's even better
you telling, him understanding how, oh yes,
their father ditched you for someone prettier,
dumber, no not ditched he's far too gentle
for that, besides he did you a service really
(most days aren't you passing the test?).
Besides they just ran off a few Ks north,
so he's reliable, their father's that
and she is too.
Who hasn't *baggage*?
We're adults, parents, have these relationships.
'Relationships?' he replies. 'Good ones. Bummers.
One particularly mean bummer.'
And nothing's wrong
in being coy re. whom he's fucked. But why?
You soon surmise what they and you possess:
lean, tanned *Been through much but gettin' my*
shit together faces, psyches still sucker for
the lesser drugs, too much drink some nights
and men, men who arriving single with a guitar
read heaps more than you do:
Hunter S. Thompson, *The Old Man and the Sea*, *Catch 22*.
Surely he won't bring out jealousy and malice?
Someone though, thinking she might be a friend
needs to warn you: 'Hang loose?' she says,
'He hangs unhinged. Why'd he finish here?'

A man can't hide from what was last year's news
in certain parts of Melbourne.
Bugger any e-highway, it's that slow-marching
seep of gossip that will out,
finding such places no digit, no keyboard, no mouse
ever reaches. You and your rough diamond?
Forget the clichés.
                    But your response is *No*
it has to be. You pride yourself in knowing men,
in holding back and choosing one who mixes,
won't overrate himself, holds the grog,
isn't a head or freak of any kind. No no no no,
he's a burley, stubbly muso in his thirties
who really likes you, whose taken to your boy
and girl with just that touch of necessary distance.
And he's moving in.

—

You know he has a daughter,
but how the child is missed, that was the clincher.
Though when he talks about her he blames
not the ex, not the other ex,
but *that* ex, the Central Victorian one.
'So,' says the man, 'let's plan it.'
And getting out the map just won't relent:
down to Bateman's, up across the Monaro and the ACT,
through the Riverina, down to the Murray

and over to that vague, orchardy area round Shep,
then west to Bendigo and south where someplace
in the Goldfields they'll be, they'll have to be:
his princess and her mother the bitch.

True that's a bit too much,
you can cope but, believing all you need
to do is calm him, and tonight's options range themselves:
certain medications, yoga, massage, massage and where
all of that might finish, and always after
you'll become that lady who can say
Yes, we'll do it, not right now of course
but one day.

And it works.
Saturday evenings at the Bowlo you beam at
the BBQ, the mellow dope, the mums 'n' kids,
with him there swaying through his pick-up
jam sessions *Taking it from the very top.*
Why even those sour hedonists
in at the bar staring at their League
seem neutral. Nobody deals, everyone shares.
That afternoon, until you went to get
your children from their dad you both
Bet you can't…bet I can again
played dares in bed.

Are you going to love him,
allow yourself to love him? Those friends
still trying to work it out
(warning you about him? more you about yourself!)

don't get it right.
    Sunday arvo should be even better.
In the beer garden your boy's made friends
somewhere, your girl's as ever clingy,
but happy.
                Then he joins the cover band
and during a set, whilst you're distracted,
gets annoyed, smiles of course,
but after the break he won't return
and stays annoyed.
                        What did you do?
What did you say?
                        Nothing he keeps telling
nothing. It's those pricks in the band.
Full stop. They invited him just
to make him look…well you saw
how he looked.
                    You can't tell him what
you didn't see. Which is right
and a mistake. And right. And a mistake.
    In a week you've said something and he's said
'Why'd you have to say *that* stupid?'
Then, whatever sense is left in his head
seems to swerve out in the wildest arc to hurtle back
and disintegrate.
                        You name it he throws it
(isn't *that*, it's said, what women do?).
So calm him, get him sheepish again.

With a little sweet, sexy affection
let's get him talking about himself,
ask when you can 'Why'd you do it mate?'
And loving explanations he replies: it's the daughter,
he stuffed that one trusting her mother;
whilst you're relieved your god's still present,
the god of *Please never do this in front*
of my children for one day that god
mightn't be present.
                        Stoned, drunk, both or
none at all, what was he today?
Sure this afternoon you're sick of each other,
still but let's hit the Bowlo.
He smiles and sways of course, whilst you remain
too taut to flirt. Didn't he announce
'I'm a one lady man'? More than ever he is.
    He's fun, he's talented, believes you've both a future
and the kids jump into his lap. Nearing midnight
you might be listening to Chet Baker
or he's reading aloud from Neruda or
The Mersey Sound.
                        Then someone says something
his mind will not be clear enough to process.
They have a target, he's the target.
You better believe him, go on say it.
But this is your home and you'll say
what you like.
                    He won't hit you, yet;

just takes an arm, pushing it up your back
to ask 'And what about what *I'm* feeling?'
You've known him how many months
so what are *you* feeling? How about
Sorry mate, just don't quite get it
or more likely *Am I to blame?*
Well I never deserved this!
Or even
This isn't how you fuck.
For some nights it's still that good, he knows it is,
something has to be. And it isn't that
he's crawling back, it's worse:
he's like it hasn't happened.

—

His screaming's recommenced. The kids are home.
And you are bruised, walking-into-a-door bruised,
like you've seen enough before except
now it's his, his bruise and possible fracture.
You saw the good man (if nobody else did)
the one who rolled you your White Ox,
the one who actually wrote songs,
the man you were loving who disguised
so much (no doubt from himself).
Well, it all is out now with a sort of noise
that's heading to your kid's guts
to stay for decades. But it's when

he starts up ‘Don’t you get it, I love kids,
I love them!’ you grab yours and lock away
the three of you, three hearts deranged
with thumping, with him outside the toilet
howling, whilst you phone your girlfriends.
    Men arrive, and now he screams at them:
the Bowlo band, the cover band, the busking partner
who then reaches for what you never thought
you’d reach with him: cops, their AVOs.
Oh, and you’re reasoning again,
he was never thick, some cops are truly thick
and sometimes we need what the thick provide.
    Meantime he’ll be off,
a stocky, perspiring man, making noises no one wants
to understand, getting dragged away.

—

    Blue-eyed handsome, by-the-book neutral,
with blonde hair in regulation buns,
when the women mention you by name,
that name he cried every time (you’re fearing now)
he loved you *They’re on my side*
you start to think *they have to be.*
    You say: ‘Domestics must be
your very worst, right?’
                                        They say:
‘Shall we send for the children’s father?’

And you have to ask for a repeat,
you can't quite get what they've said.
    They point to your face:
how will you get this attended to?
    You have the answer:
your best friend in the area's a nurse.
    You want to stay indoors? You'll stay indoors
for days because you've planned enough,
you've planned too hard.
This could've worked except he's sick
and stupid. *Once is a shock,*
twice you're a failure, but three times
that's a pattern and three times mate,
matey, sport and Sonny Jim you're out.
Oh by the way that *was Number Three.*
Hadn't grief disposed of your bravado
you might've said it.
    Whilst you locked yourself away
the Bowlo's kicked all hippies out.
By now it's spring. Whatever's replaced League
the sullen bar is staring at it.
They may be grubby, certainly are trash, but none's
as violent as he is; and if you hear *Closure*
once again you'll snap anything in half,
knowing this sound's simpler:
He's off to find another fool.
    The women cops arrange their closure
but he doesn't make a time to apologise

he makes a time to explain.
Some might say *Get into anger management mate,*
right into it whilst others sneer
You are a weak, weak man.

You, though, make a time to hardly listen,
just to be assured they're heading off now:
sheepish him, his reading matter and guitar
through regional Australia.

Memoirs of a Ceb

1

...it happens quick and (even stranger) smooth,
for it's a suggestion, a suggestion which you follow
from a slightly oiled, brush-backed man,
with just that few more years of life about him,
who may have read some books and starts by sneering 'Goose'
at you, this year's smug term of derision.
Later of course you'll need to wander home, more than
half-hoping it had happened.
Back, forth and back
Peter as server glides before the altar
where midway (this much ritual suffices)
he'll nod towards the cross. Auburn haired,
freckled-pale Rod Laver style, this is a sixth former
who'll become an engineer, sing tenor in
the University Chorale and being a true Ceb,
in keeping with Holy Trinity's Outreach Program,
has tried connecting with a neighbouring Estate,
where recently some bodgie contemporary at first
belittled him, which honing his self-deprecation
Peter still acknowledges and bears.
But where
in Holy Communion has the Rector arrived?
And as Peter looks out he can't recall any
of his motions, and so assumes that God
or an equivalent has walked him through them.

'They aren't heathens,' the Rector advised his Program,
'but if some don't appreciate, thinking that they
despise you…make friends, just as your saviour would!'
Yet what do you do when turning the other cheek
you feel somebody's mouth against it?
And the mouth is saying
'Christ Goose, this isn't going to be a bashing!'
The flat seems neat; half a dozen LP covers
are pinned at arty angles, whilst there
on the bathroom door a full-breasted floosy,
who makes you coy, might well be saying:
'Don't know what *I'm* doing here…you though
want to run off just to return…correct?
Oh yes, and what if our bodgie friend,
taking Outreach to heart, turns up at a service?
Or Cebs?'
Peter doesn't have the kind of faith
that sends you to damnation, just a one
which cultivates embarrassment. He arrives he leaves
he arrives he leaves. Were they friends now,
friends of that strangest kind who had to stop?
For there at his door 'Come back Goose…'
the bodgie's pleading, 'Who cares anyway?'
For he's crying and yes the bodgie cares.
'Knockbackers,' as the Rector urged,
'forgive the knockbackers.' But what if (as Peter knows)
one of them in some weird way is you?
'God, eh…' the bodgie would say and

'I wouldn't mind it in the army…' and
'All this? I never really think about it…'
muttering with such a low key conviction
Peter fears he could never use.

For though he still accepts
that yes, a God might yet exist,
Peter's found believing less, much less.
Or else you could be turning pacifist
but need someone (the Rector? hardly the Rector)
to help you prove it.

As for the matter of men,
how could you even mention the men?
These are such things to barely ask your parents,
though why not corner your sister or brother
and ask them stuff: the God stuff or war stuff,
the men stuff! Simply to see it in their look
Peter's thinking that?

But too much
or never too much things needed asking.
So why not 'Doc' Dalzeil,
churchwarden and flamboyant medico,
though how he had accepted the God part
bewilders Peter. If not engineering surely
science was enough?

Yes science will be enough,
for science has those hormones you've read about
and need.

And this Sunday morning

serving with the rector, Peter sees him
and knows that afternoon he won't goose off
to the Estate, but as one rational being
visit another: that one at present bellowing some
Hymn Ancient and Modern!
                                                  After which:
you'll re-believe in God, prove how, somehow,
you dis-believed in war, and beyond all these
cure your Ceb despair, by getting hormones, that
injection of hormones.
                                          And with heart thumping
more than on any Estate see Peter
blundering through a front door and out to the back yard
where the only sane man remaining in the world,
Dalzeil M.D. is playing
One two three, kick! One two three, kick!
Pied Piper to a conga line of kiddies!
                                                            'Peter?
Peter! Come right on in, my daughter's turning eight!'

—

He might serve the Rector, but looked at closely
doesn't seem to pray. Later though Peter will attend
that junior partner service, Evensong,
where he sits hearing a minister attempting relevance,
which has Peter thinking about his very recent friend
crying *Come back Goose…*

At first he felt very little,
but soon was learning that if he was hurt then he could hurt;
and now, set in this ludicrous mid-point innocence
some place between the tragic and *who cares...*
he was stepping away:
hoping his doctor hadn't got the whole thing incorrect.
Still, hormones or not Peter
whatever he's been, is and is becoming, knows he'll be
a reliable, efficient engineer.
This evening he wants to trust *that* much,
in a tired building for a tired faith which,
after seventy years is much more like a chapel,
best viewed in the dulling light of late June dusk,
sharp westerlies completing the weekend.
He looks around to read the plaques
in all their must: long-serving deaconesses,
Great War fallen, a canon and his beloved spouse.
Four square it may seem but tonight,
like some quick-fade acquaintance it simply creaks
Aw come back Goose please come back Goose.
Even with a congregation the place looks empty.
One day soon they'll flog it to the Greeks.

2

He was twelve
when father asked that Peter learn the squeezebox:
Jealousy, *Tico-tico*, the rest of those la-la-la
war horses, with some uncle forever insisting on

Piccolo Pete.

'What adolescent,' friends later sighed,
'was ever so phlegmatic, so no-adjustment necessary?'

Dad had thought his son would love to be requested,
which Peter supposed he was; or else
you just lived with this as you lived through
Mum's endearing flaps, as yet again her low-grade bigotry
got re-ignited: 'Opinions matter, mothers do what
they've always had to. Authorities are useless. As ever.'
Like when in First Year he brought home *Farrago*
just it would seem to have her confiscate
their contraceptive guide.

'How old was she?'
Cameron had asked within a night and day
of meeting Peter. 'Piano accordions
can be accommodated, and yes I know
supportive parents are a worry, and yes
I never came from Ascot Vale but
in O little town of Bentleigham
with our tiny touches of Bentleigham Bohemia
everybody knew what everybody knew...'
(though whatever it was Peter had to know,
wasn't it mostly Cameron's finely-tuned hyperbole?)

They were twenty six,
it was a warm spring evening,
and as if some minimally debauched emcee was
'Introducing...camp young professionals...
the very next stage of your existence...'

they first met at The Star, a genteelist dive
where all you seemed to do was sing-a-long
with a chorus line of J. C. Williamson fruits,
who patted you on your back and called you 'laddie'.
A pick up bar? A put down bar!
Though not that night, their night.
    ('Why'd you go there, Peter?'
    'A friend convinced me it was safe…
until I met *you*.'
                    'Whose place did we
retire to?'
            'Yours Cameron, that flat on
Beaconsfield Parade.')
    There has to be that moment when
long hours of flesh evolve to *What,*
haven't we had enough? Here came their moment:
five a.m. with Peter speaking via some funny drug
(and Cameron hearing via same funny drug)
'I was first seduced on Holy Trinity's
Outreach Program. He was some bodgie set
on calling me Goose and even worse
wasn't I almost still a Ceb? Hardly knew
what we were outreaching for except
I found too late what I'd overreached,
not that the Rector or anybody knew
other than Bob Dalzeil who saved my life
and the counsellor, we mustn't forget her, after which
I turned out an engineer.'

'Drug 'n' all,'
thought Cameron, 'he'll always be a trifle churchy...'
and you could of course imagine his new friend
seated in a pew or wherever churchies sat;
what though of Peter's tumble-dry recital with all
their remarkable words and personnel:
Goose and the bodgie, out-and-overreaching,
a Rector, Bob Somebody, ditto a counsellor,
how he became an engineer (which made a sense)
though as for Ceb (which sounded like some fizzy jube)
you guessed they all cohered, to what though?
'Peter,' and Cameron paused concerned.
'I'm hearing the weirdest kinds of psalms,
of prayers, slow down O Christian engineer,
slow down!'
He did, they both did,
and after sleeping well into the afternoon
they walked along the bay to Elwood and return.
Six, seven, eight, nine years before
there never was National Service for Peter,
it had been conscription; and how much God
can the Universe take anyway?; and beyond these
there was that bodgie and what they'd done together:
'the men stuff', he called it, knowing how
once that was solved, universes could accommodate
the rest.
'Imagine, Cameron,
you're on an Outreach Program and you are,

and you knock on the wrong door
which you do, which also doubles as the right door
for it is, with this man, older than you though still
young enough, who names you Goose
and you keep calling because Cameron you need to return
and you needn't imagine anything else, not now.
Where'd I hear hormones would cure *that*?
Time, *The Bulletin*, *National Geographic*, something
someone muttered at school?
Hormones? shouts my GP friend
The boy is asking for a shot of hormones?
Who stares then smiles and *Peter* sighs
it hardly works that way, and even better
there isn't any 'way'.
No? I plead/ half-plead.
Never he replies. *Get used to the fact*
that nothing's 'wrong'. Better not tell the Rector, though.
And *Welcome once again* I'm sure he thought
to post-pubescent follies.
But he was so enthusiastic
for me *You need to talk about it talk about it and*
talk about it so pleasantly demented.
In a few days I was to see him, he'd have made
arrangements.'
Two young men, one slightly shorter, leaner,
auburn-haired, the other slightly taller, broader with
a widow's peak, turned and ambled north.
'Who do I tell this nonsense to? Not everyone.'

'You should hear what *I'll* confess.
Does it matter I never was a Ceb?
'It would if you were.'
Over blintzes,
when Cameron asked his friend to stay the night,
both knew quite soon he'd be moving in.
Spring still holding, on the walk back
couple-upon-couple were being scrutinised:
'How long do you think they've known each other?'
'How long have we?'
'Almost an entire day!'

3

New Year's Day 1987, with little to happen.
'Little…' Cameron had moaned that morning,
'please make that nothing…' with him, Peter,
Viv and Dennis, Liza and Donald, plus the twins,
plus weighing in at eighteen months, 'His Honour',
holidaying at Viv's Dad's Fairhaven beach-house.
As they lay on the sand,
waiting for Cameron to emerge out of the shallows
with the children, Liza told Viv how the twins had thrived
at the local Toddler-Kindy-Gymbaroo and how too
would 'His Honour'.
And here was Cameron,
loping knees up out of the Southern Ocean
trying not to fall back. Soon they'd climb the dunes,
crossing the Great Ocean Road to the cottage where,

as it always evolved, the hour would turn to story time.
    And if he'd told his one for years now,
Peter as Ceb, Peter and the bodgie, Bob Dalzeil
'The man who saved my life', hadn't they all told stories:
the destruction of somebody's blender;
the boyfriend atrocity who gave everyone a photo
of himself for Christmas; how the household had to get rid
of 'users'; Viv 'n' Liza bumming rides through
Afghanistan, Iran and Iraq, as if it were a trip to Geelong;
that giggling couple, true children of the Seventies,
who thought they'd make their fortune out of quiche.
    Whilst Peter knew that some time prior to dinner
the story would he his.
    'Cameron calls that counselling institute
the Wellness Centre, as if there were any wellness centres then!
What was it? A tolerant place that wasn't home,
which I certainly required (likewise a bodgie's bedroom,
the Dalzeil backyard, The Star). And mightn't we need
that accidental someone who'll rescue us as Bob Dalzeil
that great loud man did one afternoon he thought he was
Xavier Cougat? As Cameron would rescue me
from the beats, yes him my great and even louder man...
well it could've been me blundering around,
imagining I was passing for discreet.
And didn't that bodgie save me from
some part of my hormone-deprived Ceb existence,
whilst another man saved me from the bodgie?'
    Sometimes of course the story bored him now:

Oh if one must have memories and memoirs
(and who doesn't?) shouldn't one be
proud of them? Who needs a life's reminder
I was Goose the Ceb?

And though he knew it for a good, good story
Peter had near cringed when Viv, dear Viv asked
'What exactly is a Ceb?' Thankfully her husband knew
and sensed a spot to place his arcane Cebbing baggage;
if sometimes you needed a lawyer, well Dennis
was your lawyer: who could declaim as if he were addressing
not mere jurors but the full High Court.

'Before it was the Anglican Church of Australia,
that entity as we know it now,
I want you to imagine... pause...
The Church of England Men's Society... pause...
The Church of England Boys Society!
(double pause for a stand-up comic *Get it?*)'

And the world's beigest acronym? Sure, sure, sure
they got it!

'We called it *club*,' sighed Peter,
'all British Bulldog with a pinch of prayer.'

Which had to be some time ago, who'd want all that
last week? It's sequel still felt 'last week' though,
and that was fine: how Doctor/call-him-Bob
had asked his counsellor friend to see young Peter.

Problem: how to meet her once a week without
your mother knowing? Solution: the woman worked
beside the library and each Thursday evening

Peter headed off with books there, didn't he? Risks?
Yes there were risks: who/what has more power
than children and their secrets? Only adults in their
bewildered tolerance *Sure, everyone's different…*
just not that *different!*
                    'You mustn't feel,' he had to tell
his friends, 'the counsellor gave permission to think
Nothing will stop me now! I never thought exactly *that*.
But nothing did! Sure I was *trade*,
all through Matric and beyond: if hardly *rough trade*.'
    And he told them how
The Ceb is back, back on the Estate,
talking to a man, yet another man,
if feeling silly as his mouth dries. Correction:
he doesn't 'feel' a thing occurring yet,
though isn't it still exciting, which is why he's here
(Outreach Programs, eh?). Easy really
if this and this is done this follows,
since all those last times that and that
and that occurred, go on go on guess the results!
    'Call it,' hadn't the first one said,
'your education, Goose…' a man (though you couldn't
sense it yet) much more scared than you
could ever be, for if his mates found out
guess who'll be the goose and guess his education.
    'Call it,' Peter would have told him now
'dealing with the fact there's nothing wrong.'
    Funny how it had been a secret, once,

even if he had to tell a doctor, a counsellor (if hardly
a Rector!) or some man you'd meet one day at The Star
who'd never leave you. Now everybody knew, so when Liza
announced 'A-ha Peter, your secret's safe with us...'
you only replied via bemusement:
'I barely know what my secret is!'

'Yes, secrets,' Donald admitted, an angular,
ginger-bearded man whose knowing awkwardness
helped to tell the following:
'One lunch hour, taking a shortcut down a lane-way
to the tram, I saw them sitting in a rear driveway,
two school girls, Genazzano school girls each
in the other's arms. And I see (no make that feel!)
that tremor running through them, the one they're sharing
with me: one of the world's more natural surprises.'

'So,' mused Cameron, 'were they doing-doing
whatever it is good girls, Catholic good girls do?'

'Cameron!' mocked Peter. 'Apologise!'

'I'll do more than that, you'll see, you'll see...'
and dinner time returning from his room presented...

—

Out the back of Genazzano
where, constructed like Meccano,
there's freely standing or detached,
with sleek-tiled roof near-hinting thatched,
just as the builder man remarked:

'A place to get your oldies parked.'

Now though their doddering occupants
twilight-homeward have advanced,
and smart young femmes with mock grimace
are signalling 'I need more space…'
and dusting off their welcome mats
are taking o'er these granny flats.
Whilst surgeon dads and lawyer dads,
who doubtless once were Xavier lads,
trust that the local jocks 'n' rorters
won't put the hard word on their daughters
and swiftly, for such suite be tout,
sneak in for a midnight root.

But though for most the option's boys
let me present a subtler choice:
consider such (I know you're learnin')
as those who take delight in spurnin'
Achilles, Hector or Apollo
and plunging full-on Sappho follow
down laneways every lunchtime when
they circumvent the Rules of Gen,
since hormones somehow seem to click
in what we used to term Matric
(though one per cent turn out as nun).
O such adulthood begun:
all vistas vast all limits few
for Catholic gels o' leafy Kew!

4

Can you hold court and still be in a hospice?
Can you be in a hospice and still hold court
autumn 2006? You can if you're Cameron.

Here's how he expounded: 'That's him:
the one staring at *Al Jazeera* with the sound off.'
And here's how he expanded:
'You ask me why news-cycles have become
that instant clichéd twenty four/seven? Because my chums
we even dream the stuff, dream it now and little else.
Peter, remind us of those times when there were
positive stories: like how you were a Ceb
and kept returning to that lady at the Wellness Centre;
or the Outreach Program at the Estate
and all those men you met there.'

'All? All? Just two, just two. At that age,'
relived his friend, 'someone's always taking you
by surprise (even if it's yourself).
And no, not the bodgie, he was gone to where
queer bodgies go to straighten out themselves.
But he, the real he came to see me,
and the University Chorale belting forth *Zadok the Priest*
so that in the Town Hall, balcony or stalls,
a man with a college cut who manages a hardware store
is out there asking and answering
So where's Pete? Oh there's *Pete*!'

'Someone's
always there…' and Cameron's mode turned a self-

deprecating worldly wise. 'Why, at home
a few months back, the door is knocked and here's
a single Mormon, who has lost his brother Mormon,
cute still if cute's your word. So now's my turn
at belting forth *Salt Lake City here I come/*
Where I should've started from…
just so he can stare his L.D.S
never-going-to-get-it stare, which sure got rid of him!'

The hospice had a sun deck. Wheeling Cameron
they headed to the sun deck: Cameron, Peter,
Viv and Dennis, Liza and Donald, they and those constantly
repeatable stories that bound (and always would) them
and their friends, Peter's tale being amongst their greatest.
His Ceb-stories needn't be yours but with adjustments
mightn't they? Had Cameron that part of him available
he might've improvised half a dozen nifty couplets:
how young Peter pounded his and all neighbouring suburbs
trying to find…well after gate-crashing the Dalzeil daughter's
birthday, he had to find something!

'And if you hadn't gone?' asked Liza.

'I'd have got married, had children, cruised
and spent a life sensing there was something…incorrect?'

(And he tried telling of that benign and measured
ex-commo next door in Ascot Vale,
whose commo wife had ditched him, falling out
over whatever it was commos and ex-commos fall,
but he stopped, knowing it wasn't remotely relevant.)

'I went of course.

Things had to happen quick enough
and it wasn't just those men. Even at church
I fell in love with every second Ceb,
couldn't do otherwise and couldn't do a thing,
which goes with our package as we were
constantly reminded: certain clowns at school
talking of little else *Poofpoofpoofpoof* not knowing
the least about it...'

'Ignorance,' sighed Cameron, 'a thug's ignorance.'

And soon he'd be enrolled in Engineering
(in Engineering!) still living with this *it* as if an *it*
were some disease.

'Of course I went...'

—

'I'm Bev,' she announced. 'I gather Bob Dalzeil
said how you would never change
and why should you? Bob told correct.
Why are we here? I'll never take your words
outside this room and even better
this isn't some confessional.'

He looked at her:
short (even stout) twin-setted, if only he had known
he might be talking to some parody,
Cameron's Wellness Centre prototype,
except he *didn't* know and this was Bev,
someone almost his mother's age, hearing him say

‘Yes, I suppose that’s why we’re here.’
‘Great, Peter!’ And once and loud
she clapped, no make that slapped her hands.
‘Now we can begin!’

Mixed Business

The speaker is…

Reliable as anyone I've known,
Bob Arnold is the kind of man for whom life works
because (please excuse my sentimental aphorisms)
he loves life's work; he's lucky too, since he makes
his luck: wife, two girls, an extended back/
extended up weatherboard, the briskest walk
from Dennis station, a mum and dad further up
the Hurstbridge line.
He's never said so
but unlike me he's never let his parents down.
Can't you hear mine? *Why turn out yet another teacher*
for the state and why then did you quit?
Why'd you marry whom you did then let
your marriage rot? Or *Why* in my own phrase
that lack of any focus?
Not that I would mention it,
but when you respect their aptitude, their nous
and clearly their results, when a man does plenty
and it's all success, a friend like Bob will focus
for you: which dictum, Bob need never know,
also applied to Beetle.
Let's say someone walks by/
walks into any spot that's yours along the strip
at three or four or five pm and *Yes* you get it

today I'll score! Let's further say that this is how
that world of Beetle starts, as one windy, warm,
late August afternoon I was at his place and
this girl was there: just past attractive,
just starting to age.
                                        Sure with few days left
of hanging back I still felt detached,
though with my growing edge which told me
Take what's offered. If that girl dies
(and she may die) your man won't even care.
      I had, I have my still and centred love
of self-respect (rules which even now may rescue me).
Where though lay self-respect in the ever present *that?*
Where it was to be regained of course, that swiftest,
simplest way, the Beetle way.
                                                Those days it seemed
like every second staff room (that's where I'd been
a year before) let alone every spot along the strip
had one of us at least: happy-go-usey, slightly sad,
making and remaking ourselves ever so slightly
sadder.
            My wife had never cared for me and 'sadder',
so she quit. I'll always hate her.
She and the boy friend though, I bought them out,
aiming to live alone, which dispensing with the lot
our lot (furnishings, white goods) I did,
enjoying all that propped my pride in minimal living.
Next-to-last off the carpets came, paring me to floorboards

(with a front room facing Lygon Street opposite the cemetery)
and my invalid pension. So I shrugged,
put my place on the market and finished each few days
with silent wails to some distant god,
hating it, hating her for that little twerp I was,
so that I would catch, I *had* to catch the bus
to Clifton Hill and then wait for the Beetle tram.
Until that summer's day I saw the man who sent me there,
Big Mike on the strip announcing 'Beetle's? Don't exist now.'
And I'd be best advised it never had.
Except it had.
And I thought of us: retailers, clientele, those stickybeaks-for-now,
as kids jostling in line with Skunk, Keno, Des 'n' St-st-stu
at Mother Beetle's tuckshop, big-noting sure,
though most days more big-noter wacky than big-noter paranoid:
like Skunk announcing 'Wanna join the army so I can give
the officers head!'
'Well,' Big Mike sneers, 'somewhat possible
isn't it? If he can get away from Beetle. How can he but?'
Not with the quiz-master himself
(our one with all questions, answers, prizes) reminding us how
hadn't he been Cap'n Midnight's two-i-c? and how
'...for a year whilst we were flogging his little bags o' joy,
the ol' Midnight, wasn't he the Pope!'
Well, Beetle taunted,
weren't our wishes always jelling, jelling,

to be part of such a pedigree? But in some Reservoir back street?
Never for our Cap'n! Which made me wonder
why indeed for our Beetle? Not that I need ask,
since this is what Beetle ultimately does:
forces you to imagine. I know I had to.

This sure is useless bastard weather…and near midnight,
stone-bored with these past two days of northerlies
Des 'n' Stu watch wogs on Elwood Beach wrap up their soccer.
And even if tomorrow's Sunday, Sunday can be work for some
like Des 'n' Stu: sitting it out, staring at videos, listening yet again
to Beetle and agreeing with him how Dæmon's been
a very stupid boy. Tonight but, they've credit enough with which
to hit the Crystal Palace, to choose and pay (which gets as innocent
as they shall ever be).

Welcome to Beetle's,
this useless bastard summer Sunday.
It's some place which, though boarded up,
may've passed for a milk bar, where
through that rich twenty minute glug
of video trailer voice-overs, he's been phoning.

Then when he's finished and the order's 'Kill it!'
his boys understand their choice. Beetle or the feature? What choice?
Not when he's chosen how this afternoon they're getting Dæmon round
just so these very stupid, very stoned and very minor dealers
(Beetle, Big Mike, Skunk, Keno, Des 'n' Stu) propped by Beetle-rules
can kill him, correct kill him, Dæmon a thirteen year old
user-dobber-thief. Well that's the Beetle option and if his boys
are out, right out of it enough, this will be done.

The kid's brought in
and all is prime for Beetle versus Dæmon time, how:
'It was you, wasn't it sent those fuckers round to bust us?'
'Shit Beetle-mate, that *wasn't me!'*
Which might be answered
Who then but? *except everyone's got so distracted by some boy,*
some boy who's hardly entered high school
calling their mate Beetle…Beetle-mate? Go on, try believing it!
'Hey Beetle-mate,' Stu asks in nervy spite,
'c-c-can't we start the feature now?'
Dumb beyond useless-bastard-useless,
you never had the energy to fast-forward anything.
You've been superseded by this grand stoned silence, Beetle as thinker,
who pauses, once, twice and then orates.
'He gets tied up.' Beetle stands.
'And gets put there…'
And where is there? There, there, there!
Underneath underneath! *Underneath where Beetle's jumping!*
'Feed him dog meat, feed him dog shit, anyone of you
know any better?' Of course they don't. 'And let it be wayout,
right Des? Right Stu? And by right *I mean*
so real-real wayout, beyond mere real wayout, this'll be
Return to Wayout City *and St-st-stu that's not some video.*
Correct Keno?' Who always keeps on nodding 'Correct, Skunk?
The day has now commenced and we are made for it!'
Not quite Big Mike. Earlier that arvo,
once he saw this Dæmon thing unfolding (as if he'd stay
around for *that*?) he left. They were mental. And, either on it

or not, today's product sure was. *Yep, on yer bike Big Mike*
he told himself, shuffling like he was in some folk dance
sideways to the door *on yer bike, we're relocating*.
And he had to since with all of his dealer's skills and effort,
the product and the risks, obedience was the only other option.

'I've taken risks,' Beetle would announce, 'such risks
none will understand.'

Who then murders some prepubescent user so that him and
his Beetle gang of pro-dealers, amateur killers get caught,
and for a few days' worth of summer news they hog it.
('Off the record,' a spokesman said, 'the underworld is shamed.')

And I knew them. But also knew myself:
that if it had been necessary I might have been there
that summer afternoon in Reservoir, it might've been me
shuffling an exit with Big Mike, or else with Des 'n' Stu
giggling whilst we tried to dump the corpse
(sure hadn't done that sort of thing before had they,
the things ol' Beetz got you to do!).

For even through
that slow mania of the Beetle toll, people got to know each
other,
cooperate. ('J-j-jeez Beetz,' Stu who thought he was funny
once gagged, 'don't give them ambos t-t-too much work.'
Wherever he's been sent there's plenty imitations starting.)

And truly he unites folk does our Beetle, so that when guilt,
actual proven guilt strides in, presenting itself to sighs of joy,
with the Bench contributing each decent, hard-working Aussie's
two bob's worth, oh Beetle just listen, even the very bludging,

the outright indecent are falling one-over-the-other, just to ensure how banal you truly were.

Except *we* had to survive.

There was little like it.

Me, I was fortunate. I could still promenade North Carlton beaming to and marvelling at the Morton Bay Figs.
Beetle couldn't own me *that* much, though he still required it known
Your thoughts are my thoughts and my thoughts are your thoughts
which are
'You'll be forever Beetz the best there is.'

And it fits doesn't it,

how when I heard that him and his losers were set for judgement
I knew that I'd be seeing him this final time.
And though I liked and trusted that idea, a witness seemed required:
this friend to whom I could announce: 'Now you get it, don't you?
He's the dealer I've been dealing with.'

The trial occurred in school vacation time so I asked Bob,
who as he had been painting rooms Ange permitted one day off,
gatekeeper Ange, the wife who took me for *my husband's pin-eyed user friend, him on his invalid pension.* Let her,
she wasn't to know that for all the headaches, all the heartaches
(why bother mentioning withdrawals?) R v. Beetle was the primest
vengeance show in town, my year's grandest attraction.

We caught the train to Flagstaff which got me questioning
Just how many users train it to their dealers?
Unfair asking Bob of course, his problem if he wasn't in our
Beetle club, though come, come Mr Arnold haven't you gone
teaching

spaced on your very own drug of choice? Most probably not.
Who on any 'drug' could ever be each student's matey-favourite
yard duty martinet as you are?

One lunch hour then,

Bob is motioning to me: 'See him grinning there in his long
black coat
and big thick boots? Today's E.T I'll stand any bet is stoned...'
After which we commenced those Friday evenings when my
wife and I,
Bob and Ange fronted bistros, though even then the Arnolds
must've guessed the bit, that little bit I'd be using Saturday
to get me through a day a night, another day and night of
married life.
(I've seen her with the boyfriend once: at the Vic Market where
we gave each other a tiny nod *Go on darling guess who that was...*
my useless user ex!) And at the next bistro or the next,
just to annoy the spouse Big Mike got referenced in passing.
And *that* Big Mike? Bob knew him from La Trobe. On Bob 'n'
Mike terms?
'Near enough. A Maoist once...a teacher once...' hoping to be
a junkie once;
any fad taking him to an edge, though hardly so 'edge' you
couldn't *Oops,*
easy-does-it and adjust.

Anyone's capable, just be nice if a touch
desperate
and ask about in any suburb, any town (in any staff room!)

'Know where I can find myself a Beetle?'
Well now's our final chance to find you a Beetle, Bob,
my chance to get my final taste of Beetle, him to cop
his final shot of me.
And as if I'd conjured, here came his look
that slightest pause part way between *Well wadda ya know…*
and *Who is that prick, I think I know that prick, who is that prick?*
Though when the judge, who doubtless knew less than one
per cent of it
mentioned him by the name Ma and Pa Beetle gave their baby
Who? I briefly found myself asking *Who?Oh yes yes yes*
I used to buy from that deadshit once except that now
since anyone can deal he's not being done for dealing and Beetz...
I kept staring back, a prick enough to taunt him *Beetz,*
not anyone can kill and weren't you at very basement base
all death?
'So that was him?'
'Was him once.'
'Nice word *once,*'
said Bob.
Look Beetle, look Bob at what I was back then:
twenty nine, bound for divorce, a head-and-heartache prone
high school teacher who, one Thursday after work
approached a man I knew, that same Big Mike, who sent me out
to him, this charismatic squirt (squirtier than even me,
who'd hardly make Bob's shoulders).
'Yeah we're Beetle.
What are we doing you for?'

I told him what. Who sent me then?
And as I answered, don't say we 'bonded' though we did,
over Big Mike's snigger-producing, ever-ripening moustache,
there on a Reservoir back street where Beetle worked out of
his shop front.
'...so,' I asked my dealer, 'this was a milk bar once?'
'Mixed business,' he replied, 'just like any day.'
And who was there that any day? Taster girl, another
woman too,
one I later took for Dæmon's mother, found within a year
wailing in some park.
Though by now I had a little bag inside
my jacket pocket and having survived that afternoon
I knew that I'd survive this little bag, this anything.
And I have.
For look at what's evolved:
an even more prone, divorced, ex-high school teacher of
thirty two
trying his embarrassed 'Thanks for coming.'
'My pleasure,' Bob replies.
Except for headaches I think I'd like to think I'm clean.
Lying down though which is often, my mind remains on her:
my wife,
whose secrets forced me into mine. And I could blame that
woman plenty,
who though would listen to the blame?
Even Bob, a friend who's always heard me out would walk away.
I've seen him, down the other end of a park, playing with his kids,

and as we waved I knew his feeling in return:
There he goes, someone from then *I'd rather wasn't* now.
    And never say you've never felt that way…
driving through this heritage town who's that limping
    relocated man?
Big Mike, one Interferon day to the next. That girl must be dead;
but for each Des, Stu, Keno, Skunk who wants to make some
living-or-dead effort? Hardly me. And Dæmon?
He was a kid on the news whose parents two, two and a half
    decades ago
gave idiot name upon idiot name to their disposable offspring,
as if their Dæmon would grow into his generation's Beetle.
    Who just degenerated. For I've heard this,
someone's required to wheelchair him, King Beetle-mate with
    Aussie flag
round and around the Z Division yard, this someone being
    recompensed
with product.
                So it continues, my tick-off list of
Them them and them, those those and those till it will have happened
much too many years ago, and even these memories, our sour
and blighted memories, must surely need to cease.

Waitin' for the Viet Cong

The speaker is a recently retired femocrat.

…in this way my mother, my late mother told it:
how their elder daughter, scholarship holder/doctoral
candidate,
had disappeared and how that winter in Paris,
as chill turned flu turned pleurisy turned pneumonia,
no-one, not even her parents let alone those friends
The Collective, knew her whereabouts:
that had all stopped where and when a sad girl left
without her forwarding address.
But as if my dad decreed
She's our rebel and nobody else's
I was to be saved in a way most never could be saved,
by an establishment finding its own
and bringing her home.
'Just a few days short of death,
that's right of death…' my mother told it,
'but we set to work we did, yes everybody did
to find and save her.'
She mightn't have composed
this saga of a family's miracle, she sure was its conductor
though;
and if I still defer to certain of its merits
here's the exception: this tale she told
(eyes wide alight in their bewildered pride)

was hers, and hardly mine: the girl,
so well past crying now, who having had some breakdown
was back home with her parents.

—

If only she'd never *meant* it!
Did that woman really announce (and yes she did)
'I'd like you all to meet our elder daughter, the brilliant
Marxist–Leninist…'?
What kind of La Mama farce *was* this?
For there would be my mama, this fifty-year-old high school
librarian
trundling out to friends her Great Story: when all I wanted
was to regale her with mine: be-dumped or dump.
There is that moment when,
no matter her age a child needs to announce
Yes, yours was my upbringing, nobody else did it,
but you will never understand now, will you?
And *Understand? We do we do* came their stammering
chorus
of concern: parents, educators, clerics, whoever was in vogue
But but what of your future?

—

When I still lived with my folks I might bring
The Collective home: these were my people, people ablaze

with all that kind of courage History supplies:
every argument good as won. 'Good afternoon Professor,
meet the vanguard who'll be taking over.'

Isn't there a perverse fun
meeting those you'd love to see purged?
For on occasions Dad might take my sister and myself
to the Staff Club, as if to teach
This is no 'other half', this is 'our half',
see how we live?

Then, as they glanced my way
how I enjoyed imagining the Staff Club's condescensions:
What are *we going to do with them:*
our angry children and their amazing brains?

Not all of us. Someone from a milder faction
kept courting my sister; when she turned twenty,
he told his mother they would live together
(who shrieked then ordered them married).

Now there was a couple so willing to facilitate 'dialogue',
any 'dialogue' with any one,
a pair whose future was that much in the present
it seemed near enough the past; whilst mine
just hoped the greater stories might commence:
all those things we'd live to see happen, happening:
getting rid of Imperialism for starters,
after which anything bourgeois.

I was so adept at *bourgeois* wasn't I,
using the whole Collective-at-its-grandest-heights'
greatest label of abuse (even if that's what we were, bourgeois).

Sometimes I fear these were the last occasions it was ever
employed; the saddest fact, for what other word remotely
    evoked
our world, that world we needed to replace?
    But for all his loving pragmatism *Lies?*
I wish now I could have told my dad the professor
I can accept living lies, but we've been living games!
With *we* being our family or The Collective or just
me and the girl I'd been loving near a decade.
    And she was Antoinette.

—

    When my sister and I were still in high school
Dad took his family on sabbatical.
And in the girl's school adjacent to the Red Brick,
you might say I wanted to leave, immediately leave
except for where? What puritan like me would need
the vapid joys of Swinging London? Besides,
the Sister School, the French girls had arrived
and if I was distracted now, I was ah-so-anchored!
    This was Antoinette and I:
some enchanted evening you may see this someone
you'll wish to see again, again, again, then
fly to my side and guessing I'll understand ask
Where exactly are you from and what exactly
do they do there?
                    From then who needed any bourgeoisie,

when each was such an aristocrat for the other?
Ours always would remain an aristocrat's revolt,
the skewed truth matched by the necessary swagger.
    Thin like me without my bumps and angles
Antoinette was lithe, that gamin type made for barricades,
with her well-aimed assassin of a mind designed
so that Imperialism would be hacked and hacked
to what it always was: a big-noting fraud for
men with connections.
                                        She'd come to stay,
I'd go to stay, at sixteen I'd the best indeed the only
kind of friend I needed; and on some nights
(it felt like I could never stop)
just speaking French and French again!
                                                                        'Yes, the French girl...'
Mother never asked so much as alluded:
something you knew she knew just wasn't jelling.
What though? Antoinette may not have been polite,
she sure was diplomatic though.
This she seemed to deliver, is how we'll deal
with *them*. Well at least my dad,
who'd see me to or meet me at the boat train.
    And I recall (could I ever not?)
how Antoinette took me some place where women,
women were looking at each other and it all seemed
a matter of love. Till then I'd hardly thought like that
(she knew I hadn't) but something was making sense
and making even more sense

whenever we kissed.
                                Whilst in a room stuffy from a low fire
and his perspiration, I met her sad-eyed, chain-smoking
Stalinist father, who told us what we already guessed,
and guessing knew: that all the world which really mattered
were disposing now, right now with empires.
   Three, four, five times in six months
she and I met, loved, separated and cried
(and I was not that kind of girl to cry).
Now sabbatical over, our family was returning
and with another empire poised for its disposal,
the only world I wanted known were waiting,
waiting for Viet Cong.

—

   When mother uncovered I was 'on the pill'
(a term that dates both cause and its reaction)
our grand implosion arrived.
                                'Couldn't you,
couldn't you...' she sure had gagged on something,
'just...just...protect yourself?'
                                With what?
Whilst these I still assume are what had hurt:
she never knew I'd been to see a doctor
and that shuddering idea some stupid boy
might find her potential University Medallist attractive,
or failing that easy. Meanwhile she,

the once so ever-worldly and aware,
turned into the silliest woman I would ever know
(except of course myself).

It helped she was a fool:
though I needn't worry about that need I,
since weren't there mightier concerns?

When Paris
seemed like it had been shot out of France into
and beyond the heavens, I knew the time was mine,
was ours.

Air-mailing Antoinette,
near frying myself with jealousy at their struggles,
how they were leading the world where the world
just had to be led, whilst here I was
attempting a collective life in back street suburbia:
girls like me, lean and spectacled correct-liners,
or the dumpy ones, jolly and spread out in their jeans;
those impossibly deep-voiced boys,
or the frizzy-haired ones forever quoting Dylan
in Dylan voices as if they'd truly written the stuff;
and runaways who'd finish running on or running back;
all of it banal, ludicrous, remarkable, so that you
would wake to another day of your revolt thinking
This is beautiful for this is History
and if there's to be a vanguard, guess what, it's us,
for we are going to truly matter
and I am going to return to Antoinette.

—

Nothing I would ever do had been so planned,
so mis-planned.
Candidacy and scholarship were certainties
whilst French would never be a problem:
wasn't it all mine, not as a kind of loan
but the zealous gift which, steeled and committed,
I thought had chosen me, such being that on-cue bravado
History and love both offer.
Shy, arrogant girls,
hadn't we kept each other's photographs
'Moi sur Les Barricades', 'Me and my Collective'?
Maybe. But what hers had hardly shown
was all the ground she'd filled, she'd travelled,
which wasn't I knew mere breasts and a boyfriend.
Much worse she couldn't, wouldn't announce
Don't you understand, we're hardly like that now!
Like any liberation I needed a future.
Well here came my future folding into its present
and then refolding into its past, with Antoinette asking
'Haven't you had boys?'
I had my answer
to a different question: 'Aren't I on the pill?'
(That something to make girls comfortable and annoy
mothers.)
Then catching this right-through-me look of hers
I knew what she was seeing *Here's that Australiene again*

(some place like that) a pest from my past,
and how right now in the compost of our caprice
and paranoia, my Antoinette was truly blooming.
Who did she think we had been?
Just two young women sending aerograms
and she was probably correct. Best be bland best say
She cut me and I caught a chill
as I'd say now except all I could taste
(all I wanted to taste) were vinegar tears;
as all I believed turned pleurisy and beyond.
    In some grubby bed I lay, devastated yet proud:
At least I'm bad this *bad! Could there be a better way to die?*
With little else to appreciate, why not revel in that?

—

    Since they were after me, those who thought they
        understood;
though nowadays I'd simply say her fellow bourgeoisie
were tracking down a very sick Australian girl,
of whom they'd later say was somehow saved
by telegrams, cablegrams (they meant a lot in those days
telegrams, cablegrams) and an embassy's footwork.
    Week after shaky week I'd little else but sweated,
though now someone was saying my name and I caught that
monotonal national voice diplomacy never could dispel.
Whilst all those manner of people I wished exterminated:
governments, Foreign Affairs, specialists, flight crew, anyone
wanting the world purged of every Antoinette-and-I

were helping to lift, mend, fly and propel me
through Customs and out, school girl ruthless still.
As if that mattered for, whatever my posture
I was only posture now: graceful, graceless, remorseful,
remorseless. O you dumb and greedy little monster!

—

'You realise,' my sister and her spouse confided,
'it was their networks found you…' itemising
some of my most abhorred Staff Club names.
    But as with Antoinette the only 'catch' was irony;
when Dad thanked them on my behalf and all turned History,
    unalterable History.

—

The Collective was dissolving as what replaced it
made their own mistakes re-making ours.
I tutored then I stopped to start a new life:
policy/consultancy/policy/consultancy.
I loved somebody, I loved somebody else.
I put aside telling Mother of 'Antoinette the Sequel'
but then she died. Dad remarried so I told them,
humanism all the way.
                    'That was love.'
In the movie he'd have intoned these words
deep in a mellow book-lined den.

But being on the patio of their townhouse
he had to laugh. 'Love. It can't have been much else.
And you always were whatever you always were.'
'Taa Dad.' Then I laughed too.

We knew Struggle, we knew Truth,
Knew Hué and Hai Phong,
Served such causes in our youth,
Waitin' for the Viet Cong.
Whilst Johnson, Nixon straffed the North,
Bellowed each July the Fourth:
'Longin' for the Viet Cong to win girls,
Screamin' for the Viet Cong!'

[They grew, the thick red arrows grew,
Each downward swelling prong
(Courtesy of Fu Manchu)
Waitin' for the Viet Cong:
With ev'ry Indo–Chinese peasant
Craving his slice of Karinya Crescent,
Slaughter us the Viet Cong sure will, boys…
Better kill the Viet Cong!]

One Sunday circa ten to five
Hearing our doorbell's gong:
From parents on some arvo drive
(Waitin' for the Viet Cong).

Did they clang forth 'The East Is Red'
Those chimes which shot us out of bed?
At home with the Viet Cong, 'Hi Oldies!'
'It's a pleasure, Viet Cong.'

Some played Dylan, some played Ochs,
And others Cheech and Chong.
Whilst some just played at (said their folks)
Waitin' for the Viet Cong.
With visions packed within each spliff
Like scenes from 'Blow Up', 'MASH' and 'If…'
Somethin' for the Viet Cong? Oh save us,
Nothin' like the Viet Cong!

My sister married blissed on grass,
She wore a sarong.
(I near-to-almost missed that farce
Waitin' for the Viet Cong.)
Later, back at their bourgeois ranch
Where her spouse ran his Labor Party branch,
'Why wait for the Viet Cong?' I'd taunt. 'I'm
Wedded to the Viet Cong!'

Innocent women innocent men
Little we did seems wrong.
A stroll to the shops then home again
(Waitin' for the Viet Cong).
Went abroad copped much the same.

'Now what,' she asked me 'is your name?'
Sobbin' for the Viet Cong (boo hoo hoo)
Howlin' for the Viet Cong!

The Sarsaparilla Writers Centre

Shall we swing a little bit?
PEGGY LEE, Disc Jockey Convention, Miami, May 29, 1959

Only whoop-dee-doo songs
COLE PORTER 'From This Moment On'

There's no such thing as a new melody. Our work is to connect the old phrases in a new way, so that they will sound like a new tune. Do you know that the public, when it hears a new song, anticipates the next line? Well, the writers who do not give them something they are expecting are those who are successful.
IRVING BERLIN

You can spot a bad critic when he starts by discussing the poet not the poem.
EZRA POUND

Unlike cricket, which is a polite game, Australian Rules Football creates a desire on the part of the crowd to tear someone apart usually the referee.
Instructions for American Servicemen in Australia, 1942

Dementia has set in. I'm often standing in front of an open fridge or in another room, totally forgetting why I'm there. At 62, I was hoping that this would be my last address but now I'm not so sure. Glad you're getting SBS – every time I tune in there's a root going on in one language or another.
GRAHAM KENNEDY to Henry Gay 1996

The most important thing I discovered a few days after turning 65 was that I can't waste any more time doing things I don't want to do.
JEP GAMBARDELLA in *La Grande Bellezza*

The end will come to me when I'm in the mud hut, don't worry about that, the real end. That's the only end that matters.
KEVIN SHEEDY

Hail! Muse! et cetera.

Invocation
Abandon Art all ye who enter
The Sarsaparilla Writer's Centre!

On Certain Australian Lady Poets
Coral and Lisa, Alison and Ania:
I've half a mind to exile you to Bunyah.

A Young Girl's Farewell to her Dimwitted Portuguese Lover
Senhor João Da Silva e Cardoso,
You really are a Lusitanian Bozo!

Elegiac Proposal
Cardinal Pell
Rot in hell.

Consolation for the Days of Johnny Jackboot
How fortunate bigotry
Is never obligatory.

Art in Life in Art
Whenever I hear the term 'creative juices',
I conjure a dozen negligee'd masseuses.

Hymn of Praise

(for William Henderson)

None of my creditors
Have ever been predators.

Redneck Heroes (1997)

Driving their Volvos and Mercedes Benz:
Our David Dukes and Jean-Marie Le Pens.

New Zealanders on the Nepean Highway

See the Kiwis heading to Blairgowrie:
An equal mix of Pakeha and Maori.

Lines (Really) Showing my Age

(for Laurie Duggan)

What care I for Kylie, Kurt or Bono?
I've a Satanic Majesties…in mono!

The 1987 Victorian Premier's Prize for Poetry recalled

What you see is what you get:
Runner-up to Lily Brett.

Quatrain

(for Margaret McIntyre and David Buchbinder)

I was pretty far gone. I said something about fucking Tracy and Andrew was disgusted. When I did, or maybe I already had, I burnt the curried vegetables and shaved the hair from around her cunt.

JOHN KINSELLA *Disclosed Poetics: Beyond Landscape and Lyricism*

Through all his anti-pastoral jibber
Hark to the Wheat Belt Colley Cibber!
An apt parallel, though golly
It's a bit rough to slander Colley.

'Gender'

Men have one thing on their mind;
And women aren't that far behind.

Living National Treasures

Hyped mightier than either sword or pen
The Bunyip Aristocracy Rides Again.

All over, definitely all over

There's a bloke that y'know
A right glib so 'n' so
A gratingly populist whacker.
To hayseed kin and kith
He's one absolute myth
And the name of this dickhead is Macca!

for Sally Evans

Carlos Drummond de Andrade
Penned poems of sexual ardor
Growing old he would bask
In the size of his task
Which thank goodness got harder and harder.

for Angela Williams

When humiliation's upon ya
That's where you come in Madame Sonja
I ungirded each loin
Took a boot to the groin
And all I could howl was 'Good on ya!'

for Van Badham

A stripper there was called Vanessa
And she was the cutest undresser,
Though pre-dating such fun
She once was a nun,
Well that's what she told her confessor!

True Confessions

(for Bob Adamson)
As Anne Sexton grabbed what-it-took
Berryman squawked like a chook;
The sky fell on Snodgrass
When Lowell smoked odd grass;
And Sylvia Plath was a sook.

Magicked Away

When D'arcy Niland's novel The Shiralee *came out in the mid-fifties, the Australian film industry was in its twenty-five year coma, but such was the book's popularity that film rights were quickly snapped up by overseas interests and the film version came out barely two years later in 1957. Lead actor in an international cast was Robert Mitchum, then in the heyday of his career. He amazed many of us at home by being the first American actor we'd ever heard get an Australian accent right. It was pure art, of course; an occasional shakiness in vowel quality was magicked away by his relaxed mastery of a dry understated masculine tone.*

Les Murray in an introduction to D'arcy Niland's *The Shiralee*

The taken mile reverts to inch:
That actor, Les, was Peter Finch.

The Class of '76

(for Lynne Saunder)

That Olympics we hardly rated bronze,
Whilst boys did imitations of The Fonze.

Lines for Tranter

I've toiled for years both day and night
To be compared with Patrick White;
Now I await that apogee
When Patrick White's compared to me.

Just a...

Just a male escort,
I'm no repressed sort
To the middle-aged and lonely that I'm laying.
Tell me where's the harm
With bulked up boyish charm
Given that you're servicing not paying?
I work out every morn
And I double up in porn,
From DVD to cinema to IMAX,
When the end will come (you guessed, sport)
They'll say 'Just a male escort,
Gone with his final climax.

Prodigy Poet of Hippy Parents

Why did I write? why, talent freshly honed,
Hold forth my verse to folks, most likely stoned?
Since to entrance seemed a subconscious aim
I lisped in haiku, for the haiku came.

On the Deposing of Tony Abbott

Dumped in that ditch himself has dug,
The smart-arse Catholic schoolboy thug.

Ballade for Alan Gould

What's in a name...

ALAN SHAKESPEARE

Dear Alan, with benignest aims
(you're telling me indeed *What's in*...)
I give you not immodest claims,
nor self promotion's wincing din
(non-Alans need to bear this, grin,
unless you're one you'll never know)
our king of names demands it so:
with simple maximised endeavour
watch my ballade's blazon flow:
We Alans always stick together.

No minnows in the name big pond:
Turing, Lomax, Greenspan, Fels,
even our black sheep Jones and Bond;
the world takes note and something jells:
there's that bigheartedness which tells
we're democratic by the gallons.
just reinvent yourselves as Alans,
give the past a mighty sever
Ahmed, Boris, tip the balance,
join the name that sticks together!

Near holy writ, you know it pal,
like in a movie starring Ladd

that sheer delight in being Al:
the word gets out how, man, we're baaaaad!
Chicks just swarm to Alan's pad.
Or we're a test team lead by Border
who'll willingly obey this order
(seize the willow, whack the leather!)
in mateship pure (there's little broader)
we Alans always stick together.

Claudes make way! Move over Jasons!
We lay it wide and lay it thick.
You'd think we were a mob of masons
to see backscratching do the trick:
when poesy meets biopic
who'll play the Curnows, Ginsbergs, Tates?
Why Messrs. Alda, Rickman, Bates.
(Met any poet first name Trevor?
His lonely, untuned, tin ear grates.)
Muses and Alans stick together.

Piss off Con 'n' Don 'n' Ron,
the world has not seen lesser beaux.
Like Monsieur ('ow you say?) Delon,
there's one way for a name to go:
ditch that Edgar, Mr. Poe,
join *my* friends Alans Wayman, Murphy:
airborne, waterlogged or earthy
their word is law to end of tether.

Backsliders? Hardly! What a furphy,
both they and us will stick together!

Pettersson, Musgrave, Jeans and Price
all helped to build the Alan pie.
For kudos, though, please give that twice
since be it known that you and I
can only hold up half the sky,
and needing those who'll share our vistas
– since there's a Ms for all the misters
(Kyle has Kylie, Heath has Heather)
four simple words adorn our sisters:
Allanahs always stick together!

And since our name's the sweetest fate
here be our slogan, better, motto
If he's an Alan he's a mate.
(Who'd ever be a Merv or Otto?)
Like endless First Division Lotto
our deal is trumps, our crown is jewelled.
And furthermore all gods have ruled:
from big bang to the twelfth of never
(no need to tell *you* Brother Gould)
we Alans always stick together.

From yoohoo unto toodle-oo
your days are over Jean Paul, Lou,
our cause is a when not whether.

One l, two ls, a, e, u
(oh band of brothers! happy few!)
we Al(l)a(e)(u)ns always stick together.

Alan's Guide to Alans

Alda	American actor
Bates	British actor
Bond	Corporate crook
Border	Australian cricket test team captain
Curnow	New Zealand poet
Delon	(Alain) French actor
Fels	Former head of ACCC
Ginsberg	American poet
Gould	Australian poet
Greenspan	Former Head of the US Federal Reserve
Jeans	Australian football coach
Jones	Right-wing talkbacker
Ladd	American actor
Lomax	Recorder and promoter of blues music
Murphy	Friend, co-composer of The Stag's Song
Musgrave	Wollongong musician
Pettersson	Swedish composer
Poe	(Edgar) American writer
Price	British rock musician
Rickman	British actor
Tate	American poet
Turing	British computer scientist
Wayman	Friend since 1958

The Ballade of Easy Listening

Don't tell me that it's now all past,
stretched on our generation's rack,
and though you must recall the cast
(Morgana King, Roberta Flack)
it's farewell pap and welcome cack,
with so much AM radio
selling out to vox pop yack
where'd all that easy listening go?

Oh why obliterate James Last
or Andy Williams track by track?
'Softly please and not so fast...
after this message we'll be back...'
And so they soothed through palace, shack:
unobtrusive, beige, mel-low.
With little now but thumping thwack
where'd all that easy listening go

which played it bland yet unsurpassed?
Well look out here's that corporate hack
(tin-eared, philistined, half-arsed)
who had the gall to give the sack
to Mancini, Bacharach.
Oh Mr and Mrs Average Joe
who's 'up to here' with techno-tack,
where'd all that easy listening go?

You neither seem a punk on crack
nor some rapper's erstwhile bro:
I mean it Babe, please tell me Mack:
where'd all that easy listening go?

Ballade of and for Kevin Sheedy

I'm sure you know this Bomber riff
tempered in the West Coast wars,
for more than any urban myth
(final eights or final fours)
Sheeds is as real as Santa Claus
(anchor y' windsock, swing y' coat).
Half-time was time to settle scores
the night that Sheedy slit his throat.

Passion has no place for 'if',
let's dispense with either/ors.
Sex and footy? What's the dif?
Sheeds goes 'slit', a grandstand roars
and a blonde is asking 'My place? Yours?'
I sure sowed the wildest oat,
onto sunrise without pause,
the night that Sheedy slit his throat.

But footy ain't mere lover's tiff
for here's an aching list that gnaws:
those who whack and those who biff
and worse still those big-noting bores
who imitate the shark in 'Jaws'
or think they're cunning as a stoat.
We stared 'em down and slammed all doors
the night that Sheedy slit his throat

bending certain petty laws,
(some Eagle got on Kevin's goat).
Crazed highpoint of his Bomber cause:
the night that Sheedy slit his throat!

Memoires of a one time EDFL Seconds Boundary Umpire

for David Wearne

Oh what pride and power were mine,
with ego twice as large as Asia,
when first I ran the boundary line.

Smith and Kennedy, Coleman, Kyne;
showpony, brawler, smart arse, stager:
pride and power were *theirs* and mine;

until this came with sneering whine
'Your role is anything but major,
deadshits, son, run the boundary line...'

(like a Nazi blitzkrieg crossing the Rhine,
this six foot eight of psychotic rager
with pride and power *his* not mine)

'...so chuck in the ball, else I'll break y' spine!'
But my lunch got chucked and my face turned beiger
and someone screamed from the boundary line:

'Actors are wanted at Channel Nine!'
The captain's mum. (Why didn't they cage her?)
What pride and power I *thought* was mine
when first I ran the boundary line...

Now Read On...

Melbourne, summer, the 1990s. An Afro-Caribbean English cricketer has died, poisoned, in the middle of the MCG during the Boxing Day Test. Ron is a private eye on the case, Mollie Moomba is a Koori activist, Sir Angus Wheeler is old money Melbourne whose daughter is a lesbian and Maureen Manson is a prominent right wing bigot. Now very much read on…

Brunswick Street Bohemia was Ron's bag,
He took to caffeine like Stallone to 'Rocky'.
Then came a voice: 'A man sure looks a dag,
At breakfast with his mouth half-filled with gnocchi.
What price the Bombers for this season's flag?
Haven't we both Michael Long and 'Cocky'?'
Asked Mollie Moomba, black activist supreme,
And Essendon, you guessed it, was her team.

'So how's my favorite commie-abo-dyke?
Sorry, mate, your tolerance I'm testin'.'
Ron's ocker charm you couldn't help but like,
They'd been friends since high school in East Preston.
'There's a guest host on *Today Tonight*,
Please watch it Ron, for I'm the one who's guestin',
Mollie informed 'and though my fee is handsome,
Much better I'm confronting Maureen Manson.'

The scene moves to the Wheeler's *Emoh Ruo,*
The TV's on and there's high voltage screaming

From one of this most unlikely duo:
Whilst Manson wails Moomba sits there beaming.
Snakes hiss, dogs woof and bovines tend to moo-oh;
And here Ms Wheeler howls with 'Am I dreaming?
Mollie!' She drops her uni-racial cover.
'Father behold my last but former lover!'

Back in the days of Hendrix, Cream and Traffic,
When all of us behind the ears were wetter,
Mollie decided, somehow, she was Sapphic,
For though she liked men she liked women better.
(If I wrote grunge I'd now start turning graphic.)
Let's just say that everyone who met her
Knew Mollie Moomba stood out from the crowd:
Koori! Lesbian! Feminist! And proud!

Sir Angus stared, tugging an earlobe.
His daughter's joy grew, every second, greater.
'We met in Women's Studies at La Trobe.'
At least that's what the young girl told her pater.
'Now Manson's reaping everything she's sowed.'
For Mollie was a formidable debater,
As well as wise, an absolute Minerva
(Who found her partners through the *Star Observer*).

If not to kill at any rate to wound:
'Aren't you,' asked Mollie, 'Charlie Manson's sister?'
Like in those tests when the Poms got David Booned

It was pure war, all Melbourne could have kissed her.
With Manson's mob they knew *We'll all be rooned.*
She lined the MP up and then dismissed her:
'Let the word go forth from Katherine to Kaniva:
Some deserve bouquets, some deserve…saliva!'

Those present could hear Maureen Manson mumble,
After this barb had knocked out all her stuffin':
'Like the dead batsman, that multi-mongrel jumble,
Each 'n' ev'ryone of youse are nothin'.
I know, hee hee, who caused him to tumble.
I'm hungry, think I'll grab myself a muffin,
A berry one: straw'd 'n' blu'd 'n' boysen'd.'
But with one bite Manson cried 'I'm poisoned!'

Oh see the way malevolence devours!
Deep in coma the politician dosed.
Her face was botched (a compost heap of flowers)
Drenched in sweat she looked like she'd been hosed.
An ambulance was called. They waited hours.
When it arrived all hospitals were closed.
But such was life in Melbourne under Kennett:
Part realpolitik and part Mack Sennett.

The Barassi Variations

The Argument: I've met Australian Football's most famous personality a few times and on one occasion he told of a brief sequence of words he had recently heard which, if it were repeated as many times as there were words, with each word emphasised in turn, its meaning would be considerably altered. Thus 'I never said he took the money.'

Theme

To versify my survey on
such alchemy as words contain,
I've thought it through and offer, Ron,
these variants to your refrain
(let's hope witty, maybe punny):
I never said he took the money.

Indignity

I'm the wrong guy. Who me blab?
Have Golden Rules gone all to seed?
Dealer, ponce, pimp, stoolie, scab:
let's vomit 'cause I loathe the breed.
Don't take us for that kind of bunny!
I *never said he took the money.*

True Blue

This man's Aussie and my mate.
You think friendship's passé, quaint?
Allow me to reiterate:
what's my line? Well dobbing ain't!
See here fuckhead, what's so funny?
I never *said he took the money.*

Calligrapher

Find the average talkback grating?
Got a voice and fancy choral?
Though when one's communicating
who's to say it should be aural?
Scrawled on parchment/ in the dunny
I never said *he took the money.*

Heavyweight

Well inside our suspect zone,
but out of order, sync and bounds,
we're looking at a Tyson clone
who could last the fifteen rounds
with Ali, Louis, Dempsey, Tunney.
I never said he *took the money.*

Vocalist

Young man hits the karaoke.
On me! My shout! Freebee! Gratis!
Talent scouts cheer. Almost broke he
nearly turns recording artist,
gets cold feet, walks out on Sony.
I never said he took *the money!*

Schoolmasters

Meanwhile with over-focused eye
pedagogues like swarms of gnats
amplify and specify
theses, thoses, this 'n' thats;
turning grammar, syntax runny:
I never said he took the *money!*

Lothario

The chauvinist rolled out his line:
'All babes love it, I won't hurt you.
Your place equally as mine
to dispose that shrinking virtue?'
Advantage seized? Well maybe honey,
I never said he took the money.

Girl Talk

It's a staple through the ages,
gold-digger teams with sugar pa.
Till in receipt of final wages:
'With men I'm through so ciao 'n' taa.'
Goodtime gal turned out quite nunney.
(Although of course she took the money.)

Freely and with the appropriate sense of space

Dreams: lived, dreamt and composed for Ken Bolton

1

A loft on the US West Coast. Out of a window the sun sinks into the Pacific whilst Charles Bukowski is reading in Catullian mode. 'Hey Catullus, you cocksucker! he emotes. I tell him he is a fraud but an amiable fraud, the Rod McKuen of Skid Row. He replies that no-one has ever spoken to him like that and thus he respects me.

2

It is an overcast day and Peter Skrzynecki is digging in his backyard as his neighbour Judith Beveridge looks over the fence. Peter glances up. 'Hey Judith,' he asks, 'you dig?' Thinking this some kind of innuendo Judith announces she is going to call the police. They never arrive. Peter keeps digging.

3

I am in a Chinese restaurant with Geoff Page, Alan Gould, Les Murray and an Anglican bishop (in mufti) who has written a life of Harold Holt. Murray and I sit next to each other, both ordering a 'Num Duck'. A lot of the conversation is about Harold Holt. I consider telling them about the weird sequence on the former PM written by my one-time student Jason Gunst (which was nothing like the Holt I recall!) but instead tell them of Monash student Mick Cahill telling me in 1968 'Ah they were on acid. I know some of that crowd and they were all on acid.' Then Murray stands up, tells some kind of gag and does a strange little dance.

4

In Labor's stunning return to Government Geoff Eggleston and Shelton Lea are elected members of the Federal Parliament. But whilst Geoff is content to be a humble backbencher Shelton's ministerial ambitions are stymied by the PM, who tells him that because of his rather colourful past he won't make it into Cabinet. Still, they are willing to offer him the post of Speaker. 'That'll do me, brother,' says Shelton. The Liberal members are a bit bewildered by Speaker Lea though the Nationals are seduced by his rough-hewn charm.

5

I am on a plane, daylight outside. All is quiet, too quiet. As if in preparation for an exam every passenger is reading the same Bryce Courtenay novel.

6

John Forbes, Gig Ryan and I are in what must be a 30s screwball comedy. John (Gary Cooper?) is pursuing Gig who replies with countless witty lines à la Carole

Lombard. I am in an Edward Everett Horton-style support.

7 (for Jodie Magee)
At the age I am now I have become a barrister. It is my first case and I am defending a man in Horsham who has allegedly murdered his wife. Robert Richter QC is prosecuting and this fills me with certain apprehension. I am also anxious about the questions I will ask and how I shall address the jury. At some stage I get into an innocuous conversation about Horsham with a rather dowdy female jury member, later thinking 'I shouldn't have done that, I hope no-one finds out.' But my biggest worry centres on combining the careers of poetry and the law. Then an answer to this problem arrives in the person of Robert Richter. 'Welcome to the bar my learned friend,' he says. 'I'm glad you're here because I've just started writing poetry and I'd love your opinion on what I've written.'

8
I am in Lisbon. It is night and I am walking around with Alvaro de Campos who is raving in Scots accented English. Eventually I get to ask him 'What's it like being a heteronym?' He replies that *he* isn't a heteronym, the heteronyms are Albert Caeiro, Riccardo Reis and Fernando Pessoa, and that he, de Campos invented them. Since he has spent time in Glasgow I ask him his

opinion of Robbie Burns. I am told that Burns too is one of his heteronyms.

9

The houses are a brilliant white, the sky an even more brilliant blue and PiO is an exuberant village barber, forever singing. The villagers get him to compose songs for their weddings and he does though he won't attend the services which are run by his arch-enemy the village priest. Neither of them will walk on the same side of the street.

10

The early 70s. Allen Ginsberg and Lawrence Ferlinghetti are invited to tour Down Under but forgo the experience. Then some very enterprising literary entrepreneur achieves what one newspaper describes as 'What once was thought impossible': bringing Dante Gabriel Rossetti and Algernon Charles Swinburne to Australia. Rossetti, a quiet, gloomy man suffers from jet lag the entire time leaving the running to his colleague. And Swinburne in his green velvet suit and big red afro is an enormous hit: Bob Adamson and Vicki Viidikas meet him at Sydney Airport, sceptics like Nigel Roberts and Laurie Duggan are won over and of course the Tranters have him round for dinner. Then in Melbourne things get even more frantic. A sell out at La Mama has a massive crowd clamouring well into Faraday Street. With a near carnival ensuing the police block off Faraday at Lygon and Drummond. Emboldened Swinburne climbs onto the back of a truck and gives forth with some of his greatest hits. 'Come down and redeem us from virtue,/Our Lady of Pain.' he declaims. And in spite of, or because of him sounding very much like bad imitation Dylan his audience is in positive uproar. The Pre-Raphaelite revival is on and Australian poetry will never be the same.

11

The 50s. The lamps are down low in a large London living room for a meeting of 'The Room' a collection of poets somewhat like 'The Movement' and 'The Group'. In the garb and accoutrements of the day (pipes, ties, elbow patches etc.) they are all very earnest young men except for one very earnest young woman. One of their number reads a poem which I gather is in praise of Mantovani, this being greeted with slow smiles. Then another tells the young woman that he is going to make a risqué comment. She nods and although I don't quite hear the comment I see her smiling. How young and earnest they are!

12

The mid 70s. Sir John Suckling and the Earl of Rochester are both hip high school teachers: Suckling laid back in Phys. Ed and Rochester perpetually stoned in Art. Rochester gets upbraided by the principal for making a joke about Suckling's surname which results in the Phys Ed teacher being called Mr Blowjob throughout the school. Suckling though takes a "Yeah man well whatever..." attitude. Rochester also gets into a certain trouble by taking nude photos of Year 10 girls and boys. A decade or so later dying of AIDS he is received into the evangelical outreaches of Christendom by the Rev. Fred Nile. Two decades on from that his photos mysteriously appear on the Web.

13

George Herbert is a well-meaning 60s suburban vicar who runs a Youth Fellowship following Sunday Evensong. Contemporary folk music is played and although this sometimes bewilders Rev. Herbert he still tries enjoying it. The kids love him and call him Herbie. When a smart alec interloper tries interrupting the vicar with 'What ho, sirrah, thou art but a coxcomb and a knave!' the kids become quite vehement: 'You leave Herbie alone!'

14

Ivor Indyk and I are taking Alexander Pope on a tour of the Sydney Writers' Festival, which in this case is a kind of sideshow alley. Pope is smallish, though not the misshapen midget I've read about and this slightly bewilders me. Nevertheless I have a feeling of trust about the man, if not the situation as the Sydney Writers' Festival have not invited Pope and thus he is our special, secret guest. My apprehension remains and increases as I try recalling, but can't, Pope quotations that I could recite to the great man. When Pope is distracted by what appears to be a poetry slam in a large tent (and this too is an embarrassment) I confide my anxieties to Ivor who reassures me that Pope hasn't come all this way in time and space just to hear his own words, and as for poetry slams...well the author of *The Dunciad* can accommodate anything! And it seems he can. Coming back from the slam tent Pope has a large grin, ear-to-ear.

Gallipoli 1915–2005–2015

Bu ulkeye kimin, hangi sartlarda gelecegine biz karar verecegiz.
KEMAL ATATÜRK (attrib.)

Gemileri durdurun!
KEMAL ATATÜRK (attrib.)

Hear the way élitists snigger
over our latest Little Digger;

well funny how there's nothing said
when *I* address our living dead,

nor softest heckling intrudes
upon their mate's beatitudes.

(Yet how can I...let's clear some phlegm...
show I feel like one of them?

And how to find which words to choose
for 'Fellas, I'm near one of youse'?)

Oh that my final battler breath
was breathed beside the AIF.

When little tops a patriot
line up lads, let's see us shot!

Darwin to Cooktown via Geelong
my heart tells me where I belong:

hear it pounding beaut beaut beaut,
soundbites and a photoshoot.

Go slam shut each trendy gob,
I'll take my orders from the mob.

Ahh democratic treasure trove,
let's jet home to Anzac Cove!

Polemical Lines of a Former Sunday School Teacher

Houston, Jensen, Pell and Nile
put the Son of God on trial,

though *Love thy neighbour*'s fine as such
seems like The Man forgave too much

pagan, victim, outcast, queer.
But silence for we needs must hear

pronouncements puffing out from these
descendents of the Pharisees,

their soft soap hints, their postured rant,
their Big Man platitudes and cant:

'Who'll cast these stones upon the cursed?'
All hands arose: 'Let me go first!'

And urged in spluttering cleric mode
the cowering crowd unleashed its load,

though when their volleys downed...The Boss!
they boo-hoo'd slightly at the loss.

O ever-onward Christian troops,
too late your meagre prayer of *Oops*!

This be the feast that you've been fed
by Brian, Peter, George and Fred,

whose representing Jesus Christ:
what a con-job, what a heist!

Faith-based Solutions

for Bruce Wearne

On their Islamic double-decker
Sunni and Shi'ite zoom to Mecca.

The news they bring seems up-to-date:
Crusaders versus Caliphate.

Catholics in full production mode
are propped by their Virgin Mother lode;

yet if an icon truly rocks
that's easy when one's Orthodox.

Bug-eyed, sweaty, foaming, panting,
the Evangelicals are ranting,

whilst for those who've lost the plan
what constitutes an Anglican

take your local Swami's tip
and head to the Ganges for a dip.

The Dalai Lama needn't mope,
he's something like a Buddhist Pope,

though if Shinto aims to please
it's better you are Japanese.

Be warned! The time approaches when
the Rainbow Serpent rides again.

And wither mankind's Collective Id
should Zeus turn out the Comeback Kid?

(Partly blessing, partly curse
my Deity's the Universe.)

From Mossad to the Wailing Wall
Judaism's got it all!

Sian Gammie's Roman–Illawarra Blues

Roman nuns sure are pretty, the Virgin Mary is their queen
Roman nuns sure are pretty, the Virgin Mary is their queen
Straight, dyke or neither and those somewhere in between

I went down to St Peter's and I chatted with the Pope
It's true, down to St Peter's and I chatted with the Pope
He said *Strange times are upon us Al, ecstasy's replacing dope*

The churches are quite famous for their paintings
    and their bells
Yeah those churches are quite famous for their paintings
    and their bells
And in one there was this Madonna looking just like
    Miriam Wells

Eating out's a pastime but supermarket shopping's fine
Eating out's a pastime but supermarket shopping's fine
There's kilometres of pasta and a sea of endless wine

I went and got my mobile 'cause I felt so all alone
Yeah I went and got my mobile 'cause I felt so all alone
But whilst my girl had Optus, I was stuck with Vodafone

When my girl comes back from shopping then my life is
    put on hold

When my girl comes back from shopping then my life is
put on hold
Woman is my priority, I do everything I'm told

The Empire it had Egypt, it had Syria it had Gaul
It had those Ancient Britons don't forget that wild old Gaul
The Colosseum's mighty, I prefer the Crown St Mall.

The AppianWay was famous helping Romans out of town
The Appian Way was famous helping Romans out of town
But nothing beats that Princes Highway when it turns left
out of Crown

What this place requires is an Italian Jamberoo
Yeah what this place requires is an Italian Jamberoo-hoo!
But I'd aim for half a dozen, one just simply wouldn't do

Gammie Gammie Gammie here concludes my Roman song
Gammie Gammie Gammie here concludes my Roman song
It's much better than a doco, a girl can really sing along

For Chris Wallace-Crabbe at Eighty

Wallace-Crabbe, Chris Wallace-Crabbe,
let me the first to blab:
no reticence I must implore
since some of us just gape in awe
that you, both masterful and matey,
full-head-of-haired are reaching eighty.
Ain't it bonzer, ain't it fab,
you're still a young 'un, Wallace-Crabbe!

Wallace-Crabbe, Chris Wallace-Crabbe,
at lyric arts your hand is dab,
a lesson to all poet fellas,
in our game near best of sellers,
whose fine-tempered musings, ravings
augment our psyche and your savings:
ANZ, Commonwealth, Westpac, NAB,
let funds grow flush for Wallace-Crabbe!

Professor (emeritus) Wallace-Crabbe,
first off the rank he is the cab,
a man who's shared and never hogged
let's get his output catalogued:
five-plus decades of precision
since *The Music of Division*,
well-wrought sinews lacking flab,
this be the verse of Wallace-Crabbe.

Drink up, drink up, it's on our tab,
Wallace-Crabbe, Chris Wallace-Crabbe,
from Hurstbridge on the northeast side
to Williamstown now gentrified
and Parkville at its most urbane
says anyone with half that brain:
'Mercutio can have Queen Mab,
for we have you Chris Wallace-Crabbe!'

The Ballad of 68 or I Was Dransfield's Dealer

If poets are all so ego-damned
(it's public sport to bruise 'em)
let's echo this throughout the land:
'We've talents too, and use 'em!
The plumber plumbs, the drummer drums,
and wheelies does the wheeler.
Midwives tend to birthing mums...'
And I was Dransfield's dealer!

Bob Adamson he had a void
which somehow needed fillin'.
Guess the persona he employed:
part Duncan and part Dylan.
'Let's make the local product new!'
and up spake John E Tranter.
'We band of brothers, happy few,
will do it in a canter.'

My Dransfield was a fecund lad
who wrote ten poems daily,
till Tipping stumbled o'er our pad
playing his ukelele.
Police nicknames since they began
range from 'pig' to 'peeler'.
'Officer! Arrest that man
upstaging Dransfield's dealer!'

Poems from Melbourne's academe
truly proved a bummer,
no wonder an alternate team
assembled at La Mama.
The muse, part nun/part tart/part nurse
proved quite undiscerny,
and even backed attempts at verse
from Duggan, Scott and Wearney.

Each poem when a drug got named
I grasped this heady notion:
'That's poetry!' some may have claimed,
I knew it for promotion.
With zealotry so in the air
what zealots could be zealer?
We made a truly alpha pair,
Dransfield and his dealer.

'But hang on,' said our lady friends,
'we notice an imbalance.'
The boys rushed forth to make amends
and there bedecked in talents:
Jennifer, Vicki, Joanne, Pam,
each blazed like a supernova
to hear the inevitable 'Yes ma'm...
I guess you're taking over!'

For those were the days when we were on
a libertarian bender,
no strictures to be put upon
race, religion, gender.
I did not differentiate
twixt homo, bloke or sheila,
all humanity proved *my* mate
when I was Dransfield's dealer.

Some memories though are mighty sour
I have to hold my tears back,
they still assail me hour by hour
from over forty years back.
'G'day g'day, guess who's in town?'
I tried to act appealing,
for snarling snap and freaky frown
are risks you cop when dealing.

Hypocrisy went 'Tut-tut-tut...'
that moment it would owe me,
prevaricating 'But-but-but...'
and never wished to know me.
Thinking such notoriety
had ceased with Christine Keeler
I sliced through its mock-piety:
'You *bought* from Dransfield's dealer!'

If I shook my head to see such fools
ferreted from my care,
free markets don't need any rules
so tell me why should I care?
From sources (how can one begin?)
whose well-springs would amaze ya,
some scored their dope from Mr Sin
and some from Mr Asia.

Seeing my future more boutique
than David Jones' or Myer's,
I serviced decade, year, month, week
our bunch of versifiers.
Know how it is when the top's been reached,
you just require that sealer?
Now mine was a cachéd name they preached
as *every* poet's dealer!

Some wrote with cadenced metre, rhyme,
and some wrote in demotic,
all having with me through this time
relations symbiotic.
More leaders in our fields than led,
us eminent first-raters,
stoned off each head, away we sped,
I and my 68ers.

So much acclaimed I'm now retired
feted throughout the nation,
recall those stanzas I inspired,
the breadth of my ovation:
from poets when each rhyme scheme clicks
in verses built with metric bricks,
to playin' Bach or playin' Bix
musos with their riffs and licks
(we'll at a pinch include those pricks:
the paparazzi snappin' pix,
and those who get religious kicks
– Orthodox, Protestant and Micks –)
from Beyond-the-Black-Stump hicks
to Bogan Western Sydney chicks
(now could you get much realer?).
From Mount Olympus to the Styx,
all muses granting great big ticks:
'What would we be without you? Nix!
Great work! Dransfield's dealer!'

Ode for Johanna Featherstone & Fiona Wright

Australian Poetry Ltd is a new organisation due to be launched in 2011 as a merger between the Australian Poetry Centre based in Melbourne and Poets Union based in NSW. It will be the peak industry body for poetry in this country with a charter to promote and support Australian poets and poetry locally, regionally, nationally and internationally.
from a communication, October 2010

Industry Body, Peak Industry Body,
Deleting detractors and shaming the shoddy,
The word having gone out here come delegations
From locale and region, this and all nations:
'Have you heard?' 'Can it be?' 'Don't believe…'
'Oh my god-ee...
Our verse has attained a Peak Industry Body!'

Industry Body, Peak Industry Body,
Thou mentoring magus like Big Ears to Noddy,
As philistine ill winds grow keener and keener
O'er villanelle, sapphic, pantoum and sestina,
Now slice like a scalpel, now whack like a waddy
You scourge o' th' wowsers, Peak Industry Body!

Industry Body, Peak Industry Body,
Whilst some are smart-phoney and others iPod-ey,
On all fours we lap up the springs of the muses
And our juice of creation just oozes and oozes,

Deserving much more than a tepid hot toddy
Your top shelf awaits us, Peak Industry Body!

Industry Body, Peak Industry Body,
Though crooks may be crooked and coppers be ploddy,
Law-breakers/enforcers will quiver and quake
For little beats Passion when Art is at stake:
And we've dumped our trifecta having gone for the quaddy,
You're the winner we're backing, Peak Industry Body!

Notes

They Came to Moorabbin

AWAS: Australian Women's Army Service in World War 2

HSV-7: Melbourne's first television station which opened in 1956

XVI Olympiad: held in Melbourne in 1956

IT'S ON AGAIN: a tabloid billboard announcing the start of the Victorian Football League season

The Village Glee Club: a rather twee radio program of the 1950s and 60s

Mixed Business

Cap'n Midnight: a reference to a minor character in my verse novel *The Lovemakers*, a member of the Joy Boys Drug Syndicate.

Crystal Palace: a brothel first featured in my verse novel *The Nightmarkets*.

Today's E.T. I'll stand any bet is stoned: E.T. is a Victorian term for Emergency Teacher (as in relief or supply). This line is from my poem 'A High School Staff Room, Melbourne's Northern Suburbs, Winter 1977'.

Waitin' for the Viet Cong

Red Brick: any number of Post War British Universities

Ballade of and for Kevin Sheedy

Kevin Sheedy, Essendon coach 1981–2007 once made throat-cutting gestures towards an opposition player and was thus charged with 'bringing the game into disrepute'. I can think of any number of poetasters and promoters of doggerel (rhyming, blank verse or free) who should be charged with bringing poetry into disrepute, none of whom would ever be the Sheedy in our field.

Now Read On...

Kennett: Jeff Kennett, Victorian Premier 1992–1999, 'economic rationalist', 'libertarian' and 'real character'.

Sian Gammie's Roman–Illawarra Blues

Miriam Wells: first 'Girl Friday' of Grand Parade Poets. One of the major reasons we have produced as many books as we have.

The Ballad of 68...

68ers: a group of poets, myself included, were one named 'The Generation of 68'. Re. this silly term, we had no say in the matter.

Acknowledgements

Some of these poems have appeared in *Melbourne Subjective* (ed. Patsy Poppenbeek), *The Best Australian Poetry 2004* (ed. Les Murray), *The Best Australian Poetry 2005* (ed. Les Murray), *The Best Australian Poetry 2011* (ed. John Tranter), *The Best Australian Poetry 2012* (ed. John Tranter), *The Best Australian Poetry 2014* (ed. Geoff Page), *The Age*, *Heat* and *TEXT Journal*.

Thanks to my employers, the University of Wollongong and its Faculty of Law, Humanities and the Arts (formerly the Faculty of Creative Arts) for their support during both long service leave and study leave when much of this volume was written; with a special mention to the Faculty of Arts and Social Sciences, Kingston University, London

Thanks to the Literature Board of the Australia Council for the residency at the BR Whiting Studio, Rome, during the second half of 2009, and to Ms Lori Whiting who donated the studio for the use of Australian writers.

Thanks to Jacqui Howarth who supervised the recording of the 'Five Verse Narratives' and certain poems from 'The Sarsaparilla Writer's Centre', and to the University of Wollongong for the use of their facilities. These readings are available from the Grand Parade Poets website.

And thank you to Miss Samantha Mansell for assistance in proof-reading this volume.

The Giramondo Publishing Company acknowledges the support of Western Sydney University in the implementation of its book publishing program.